D1348554

700038976378

TITANIC

SHOWING THE LOSS OF LIFE ON THE *TITANIC*

First Class

	Carried.	Saved.	Lost.	Per cent. saved.
Men	173	58	115	34
Women . . .	144	139	5	97
Children . . .	5	5	0	100
Total	322	202	120	63

Second Class

	Carried.	Saved.	Lost.	Per cent. saved.
Men	160	13	147	8
Women . . .	93	78	15	84
Children . . .	24	24	0	100
Total	277	115	162	42

Third Class

	Carried.	Saved.	Lost.	Per cent. saved.
Men	454	55	399	12
Women . . .	179	98	81	55
Children . . .	76	23	53	30
Total	709	176	533	25

Total Passengers

	Carried.	Saved.	Lost.	Per cent. saved.
Men	787	126	661	16
Women . . .	416	315	101	76
Children . . .	105	52	53	49
Total	1308	493	815	38

Crew

	Carried.	Saved.	Lost.	Per cent. saved.
Men	875	189	686	22
Women . . .	23	21	2	91
Total . . .	898	210	688	23

Total Passengers and Crew

	Carried.	Saved.	Lost.	Per cent. saved.
Men	1662	315	1347	19
Women . . .	439	336	103	77
Children . . .	105	52	53	49
Total	2206	703	1503	32

TITANIC

FILSON YOUNG

AMBERLEY

First published in 1912

This illustrated edition first published 2011

Amberley Publishing Plc
Cirencester Road, Chalford,
Stroud, Gloucestershire, GL6 8PE

www.amberley-books.com

Copyright © Amberley Publishing, 2011

ISBN 978 1 4456 0407 7

British Library Cataloguing in Publication Data.
A catalogue record for this book is available
from the British Library.

Printed in the UK.

Contents

I

The Giant Ship Takes Shape

If you enter Belfast Harbour early in the morning on the mail steamer from Fleetwood you will see far ahead of you a smudge of smoke. At first it is nothing but the apex of a great triangle formed by the heights on one side, the green wooded shores on the other, and the horizon astern. As you go on the triangle becomes narrower, the blue waters smoother, and the ship glides on in a triangle of her own — a triangle of white foam that is parallel to the green triangle of the shore. Behind you the Copeland Lighthouse keeps guard over the sunrise and the tumbling surges of the Channel, before you is the cloud of smoke that joins the narrowing shores like a gray canopy; and there is no sound but the rush of foam past the ship's side.

You seem to be making straight for a gray mud flat; but as you approach you see a narrow lane of water opening in the mud and shingle. Two low banks, like the banks of a canal, thrust out their ends into the waters of the lough; and presently, her speed reduced to dead slow, the ship enters between these low mud banks, which are called the Twin Islands. So narrow is the lane that as she enters the water rises on the shingle banks and flows in waves on either side of her like two gray horses with white manes that canter slowly along, a solemn escort, until the channel

1. *Olympic* and *Titanic* - view of bows in shipyard construction scaffolding.

between the islands is passed. Day and night, winter and summer, these two gray horses are always waiting; no ship ever surprises them asleep; no ship enters but they rise up and shake their manes and accompany her with their flowing, cantering motion along with the confines of their territory. And when you have passed the gates that they guard you are in Belfast Harbour, in still and muddy water that smells of the land and not of the sea; for you seem already to be far from the things of the sea.

As you have entered the narrow channel a new sound, also far different from the liquid sounds of the sea, falls on your ear; at first a low sonorous murmuring like the sound of bees in a giant hive, that rises to a ringing continuous music — the multitudinous clamour of thousands of blows of metal on metal. And turning to look whence the sound arises you seem indeed to have left the last of the things of the sea behind you; for on your left, on the flattest of the mud flats, arises a veritable forest of iron; a leafless forest, of thousands upon thousands of bare rusty trunks and branches that tower higher than any forest trees in our land, and look like the ruins of some giant grove submerged by the sea and in the brown autumn of its life, stripped of its leaves and laid bare again, the dead and rusty remnants of a forest. There is nothing with any broad or continuous surface — only thousands and thousands of iron branches with the gray sky and the smoke showing through them everywhere, giant cobwebs hanging between earth and the sky, intricate, meaningless networks of trunks and branches and sticks and twigs of iron.

But as you glide nearer still you see that the forest is not lifeless, nor its branches deserted. From the bottom to the topmost boughs it is crowded with a life that at first seems like that of mites in the interstices of some rotting fabric, and then like birds crowding the branches of the leafless forest, and finally appears as a multitude of pigmy men swarming and toiling amid the skeleton

2. The funnel-less *Titanic* in May 1911 just after her launch.

iron structures that are as vast as cathedrals and seem as frail as gossamer. It is from them that the clamour arises, the clamour that seemed so gentle and musical a mile away, and that now, as you come closer, grows strident and deafening. Of all the sounds produced by a man's labour in the world this sound of a great shipbuilding yard is the most painful. Only the harshest materials and the harshest actions are engaged in producing it: iron struck upon iron, or steel smitten upon steel, or steel upon iron, or iron upon steel — that and nothing else, day in, day out, year in and year out, a million times a minute. It is an endless, continuous birth-agony, that should herald he appearance of some giant soul. And great indeed should be the overture to such an agony; for it is here that of fire and steel, and the sweat and pain of millions of hours of strong men's labour, were born those two giant children that were destined by man finally to conquer the sea.

In this awful womb the *Titanic* took shape. For months and months in that monstrous iron enclosure there was nothing that had the faintest likeness to a ship; only something that might have been the iron scaffolding for the naves of half-a-dozen cathedrals laid end to end. Far away, furnaces were smelting thousands and thousands of tons of raw material that finally came to this place in the form of great girders and vast lumps of metal, huge framings, hundreds of miles of stays and rods and straps of steel, thousands of plates, not one of which twenty men could lift unaided; millions of rivets and bolts — all the heaviest and most sinkable things in the world. And still nothing in the shape of a ship that could float upon the sea. The seasons followed each other, the sun rose now behind the heights of Carrickfergus and now behind the Copeland Islands; daily the ships came in from fighting with the boisterous seas, and the two gray horses cantered beside them as they slid

3. *Titanic* being fitted out. A special quay was located next to the Thompson Dry Dock, where this work was undertaken. Thousands of men swarmed over her as her sumptuous interiors were fitted.

between the islands; daily the endless uproar went on, and the tangle of metal beneath the cathedral scaffolding grew denser. A great road of steel, nearly a quarter of a mile long, was laid at last a road so heavy and so enduring that it might have been built for the triumphal progress of some giant railway train. Men said that this roadway was the keel of a ship; but you could not look at it and believe them.

The scaffolding grew higher; and as it grew the iron branches multiplied and grew with it, higher and higher towards the sky, until it seemed as though man were rearing a temple which would express all he knew of grandeur and sublimity, and all he knew of solidity and permanence — something that should endure there, rooted to the soil of Queen's Island for ever. The uproar and the agony increased. In quiet studios and offices clear brains were busy with drawings and calculations and subtle elaborate mathematical processes, sifting and applying the tabulated results of years of experience. The drawings came in time to the place of uproar; were magnified and subdivided and taken into grimy workshops; and steam hammers and steam saws smote and ripped at the brute metal, to shape it in accordance with the shapes on the paper. And still the ships, big and little, came nosing in from the high seas — little dusty colliers from the Tyne, and battered schooners from the coast, and timber ships from the Baltic, and trim mail steamers, and giants of the ocean creeping in wounded for succour — all solemnly received by the twin gray horses and escorted to their stations in the harbour. But the greatest giant of all that came in, which dwarfed everything else visible to the eye, was itself dwarfed to insignificance by the great cathedral building on the island.

The seasons passed; the creatures who wrought and clambered among the iron branches, and sang their endless song of labour there, felt the steel chill beneath the frosts of winter, and burning hot beneath the sun's rays in summer, until at last the skeleton within the scaffolding began to take a shape, at the sight of which men held their breaths. It was the shape of a ship, a ship so monstrous and unthinkable that it towered high over the buildings and dwarfed the very mountains beside the water. It seemed like some impious blasphemy that man should fashion this most monstrous and ponderable of all his creations into the likeness of a thing that could float upon the yielding waters. And still the arms swung and the hammers rang, the thunder and din continued, and the gray horses shook their manes and cantered along beneath the shadow, and led the little ships in from the sea and out again as though no miracle were about to happen.

A little more than its own length of water lay between the iron forest and the opposite shore, in which to loose this tremendous structure from its foundations and slide it into the sea. The thought that is should ever be moved from its place, except by an earthquake, was a thought that the mind could not conceive, nor could anyone looking at it accept the possibility that by any method this vast tonnage of metal could be borne upon the surface of the waters. Yet, like an evil dream, as it took the shape of a giant ship, all the properties of a ship began to appear and increase in hideous exaggeration. A rudder as big as a giant elm tree, bosses and bearings of propellers the size of a windmill — everything was on a nightmare scale; and underneath the iron foundations of the cathedral floor men were laying on concrete beds pavements of oak and great cradles of timber and iron, and sliding ways of pitch pine to support the bulk of the monster when she was moved, every square inch of the pavement surface bearing a weight of more than two tons. Twenty tons of tallow were spread upon the ways, and hydraulic rams and triggers built and fixed against the bulk of the ship so that, when the moment came, the waters she was to conquer should thrust her finally from earth.

And the time did come. The branching forest became clothed and thick with leaves of steel. Within the scaffoldings now towered the walls of the cathedral, and what had been a network of girders and cantilevers and gantries and bridges became a building with floors, a ship with decks. The skeleton ribs became covered with skins of wood, the metal decks clothed with planks smooth as a ballroom floor. What had been a building of iron became a town, with miles of streets and hundreds of separate houses and buildings in it. The streets were laid out; the houses

WHITE STAR LINE.

"OLYMPIC."
45,000 TONS.
AND
"TITANIC."
45,000 TONS.

THE LARGEST STEAMER IN THE WORLD.

4. White Star Line advertising poster of *Titanic* and its sister ship *Olympic* aimed at the Irish emigrant market.

M.B.B

ALL STEAMERS BUILT IN IRELAND.

QUEENSTOWN-NEW YORK
ON THURSDAYS AND FRIDAYS.

QUEENSTOWN-BOSTON
ON WEDNESDAYS.

For Freight and Passage apply to

were decorated and furnished with luxuries such as no palace ever knew.

And then, while men held their breath, the whole thing moved, moved bodily, obedient to the tap of the imprisoned waters in the ram. There was no christening ceremony such as celebrates the launching of lesser ships. Only the waters themselves dared to give the impulse that should set this monster afloat. The waters touched the cradle, and the cradle moved on the ways, carrying the ship down towards the waters. And when the cradle stopped the ship moved on; slowly at first, then with a movement that grew quicker until it increased to the speed of a fast trotting horse, touching the waters, dipping into them, cleaving them, forcing them asunder in waves and ripples that fled astonished to the

5. The *Titanic* in Belfast Lough, leaving for the short run to Southampton.

surrounding shores; finally resting and floating upon them, while thousands of the pigmy men who had roosted in the bare iron branches, who had raised the hideous clamour amid which the giant was born, greeted their handiwork, dropped their tools, and raised their hoarse voices in a cheer.

The miracle had happened. And the day came when the two gray horses were summoned to their greatest task; when, with necks proudly arched and their white manes flung higher than ever, they escorted the *Titanic* between the islands out to sea.

2

Noon, Wednesday 10 April 1912: *Titanic* Slips Out of Southampton

At noon on Wednesday, 10 April 1912, the *Titanic* started from Southampton on her maiden voyage. Small enough was her experience of the sea before that day. Many hands had handled her; many tugs had fussed about her, pulling and pushing her this way and that as she was manoeuvred in the waters of Belfast Lough and taken out to the entrance to smell the sea. There she had been swung and her compasses adjusted. Three or four hours had sufficed for her trial trip, and she had first felt her own power in the Irish Sea, when all her new machinery working together, at first with a certain reserve, and diffidence, had tested and tried its various functions, and she had come down through St George's Channel and round by the Lizard, and past the Eddystone and up the Solent to Southampton Water, feeling a little hustled and strange, no doubt, but finding this business of ploughing the seas surprisingly easy after all. And now, on the day of sailing, amid the cheers of a crowd unusually vast even for Southampton Docks, the largest ship in the world slid away from the deep-water jetty to begin her sea life in earnest.

In the first few minutes her giant powers made themselves felt. As she was slowly gathering way she passed the liner *New York*,

6. The last rope is let go at the White Star dock at Southampton and *Titanic* sets sail at noon on Wednesday 10 April 1912. Despite scheduled stops in Cherbourg and Queenstown (now Cobh), she was never to tie up at a dockside again.

7. Stern out form the new White Star dock, *Titanic's* gangway door is still open, and on her aft docking bridge can be found First Officer Murdoch and a quartermaster.

8. Passing the SS *New York*, of the American Line, the suction caused by *Titanic's* huge propellers caused the mooring rope to break and for the *New York* to be pulled dangerously close to the stern of *Titanic*.

another ocean monarch, which was lying like a rock moored by seven great hawsers of iron and steel. As the *Titanic* passed, some mysterious compelling influence of the water displaced by her vast bulk drew the *New York* towards her; snapped one by one the great steel hawsers and pulled the liner from the quayside as though she had been a cork. Not until she was within fifteen feet of the *Titanic*, when a collision seemed imminent, did the ever-present tugs lay hold of her and haul her back to captivity.

Even to the most experienced traveller the first few hours on a new ship are very confusing; in the case of a ship like this, containing the population of a village, they are bewildering. So the eight hours spent by the *Titanic* in crossing from Southampton to Cherbourg would be spent by most of her passengers in taking their bearings, trying to find their way about and looking into all the wonders of which the voyage made them free. There were luxuries enough in the second class, and comforts enough in the third to make the ship a wonder on that account alone; but it was the first class passengers, used as they were to all the extravagant luxuries of modern civilized life, on whom the discoveries of that first day of sun and wind in the Channel must have come with the greatest surprise. They had heard the ship described as a floating hotel; but as they began to explore her they must have found that she contained resources of a perfection unattained by any hotel, and luxuries of a kind unknown in palaces. The beauties of French chateaux and of English country houses of the great period had been dexterously combined with that supreme form of comfort which the modern English and Americans have raised to the dignity of a fine art. Such a palace as a great artist, a great epicure, a great poet and the most spoilt and pampered woman in the world might have conjured up from their imagination in an idle hour was here materialized and set, not in a fixed landscape of park and woodland, but on the dustless road of the sea, with the sunshine of an English April pouring in on every side, and the fresh salt airs of the Channel filling every corner with tonic oxygen.

Catalogues of marvels and mere descriptions of wonders are tiresome reading, and produce little effect on the mind; yet if we are to realize the full significance of this story of the *Titanic*, we must begin as her passengers began, with an impression of the lavish luxury and beauty which was the setting of life on board. And we can do no better than follow in imagination the footsteps of one ideal voyager as he must have discovered, piece by piece, the wonders of this floating pleasure house.

If he was a wise traveller he would have climbed to the highest point available as the ship passed down the Solent, and that would be the boat deck, which was afterwards to be the stage of so tragic a drama. At the forward end of it was the bridge — that sacred area paved with snow-white gratings and furnished with many brightly polished instruments. Here were telephones to all

9. The bridge of *Titanic*.

10. The Marconi room aboard *Titanic's* sister ship, *Olympic*.

11. The gymnasium on the *Titanic*.

the vital parts of the ship, telegraphs to the engine room and to the fo'c'stle head and after-bridge; revolving switches for closing the watertight doors in case of emergency; speaking tubes, electric switches for operating the foghorns and sirens — all the nerves, in fact, necessary to convey impulses from this brain of the ship to her various members. Behind the bridge on either side were the doors leading to the officers' quarters; behind them again, the Marconi room — a mysterious temple full of glittering machines of brass, vulcanite, glass, and platinum, with straggling wires and rows of switches and fuse boxes, and a high priest, young, clean-shaven, alert and intelligent, sitting with a telephone cap over his head, sending out or receiving the whispers of the ether. Behind this opened the grand staircase, an imposing sweep of decoration in the Early English style, with plain and solid panelling relieved here and there with lovely specimens of deep and elaborate carving in the manner of Grinling Gibbons; the work of the two greatest woodcarvers in England. Aft of this again the white pathway of the deck led by the doors and windows of the gymnasium, where the athletes might keep in fine condition; and beyond that the white roof above ended and the rest was deck space open to the sun and the air, and perhaps also to the smoke and smuts of the four vast funnels that towered in buff and black into the sky — each so vast that it would have served as a tunnel for a railway train.

But the ship has gathered way, and is sliding along past the Needles, where the little white lighthouse looks so paltry beside the towering cliff. The Channel air is keen, and the bugles are sounding for lunch; and our traveller goes down the staircase, noticing perhaps, as he passes, the great clock with its figures which symbolise Honour and Glory crowning Time. Honour and Glory must have felt just a little restive as, having crowned one o'clock, they looked down from Time upon the throng of people descending the staircase to lunch. There were a few there who had earned, and many people had received, the honour and glory represented by extreme wealth; but the two figures stooping over the clock may have felt that Success crowning Opportunity would have been a symbol more befitting the first-class passengers of the *Titanic*. Perhaps they looked more kindly as one white-haired old man passed beneath — W.T. Stead, that untiring old warrior and fierce campaigner in peaceful causes, who in fields where honour and glory were to be found sought always for the true and not the false. There were many kinds of men there — not every kind, for it is not every man who can pay from fifty to eight hundred guineas for a four days' journey; but most kinds of men and women who can afford to do that were represented there.

12. William Stead (first class passenger), a famous reformer and editor who went down with the ship. A fortune teller had told him to 'beware of water'.

Our solitary traveller, going down the winding staircase, does not pause on the first floor, for that leads forward to private apartments, and aft to a writing room and library; nor on the second or third, for the entrance halls there lead to state rooms; but on the fourth floor down he steps out into a reception room extending to the full width of the ship and of almost as great a length. Nothing of the sea's restrictions or discomforts here! Before him is an Aubusson tapestry, copied from one of the *Chasses de Guise* series of the National Garde-Meuble; and in this wide apartment there is a sense, not of the cramping necessities of the sea, but of all the leisured and spacious life of the land. Though this luxurious emptiness the imposing dignities of the dining saloon are reached; and here indeed all the insolent splendour of the ship is centred. It was by far the largest room that had ever floated upon the seas, and by far the largest room that had ever moved from one place to another. The seventeenth-century style of Hatfield and Haddon Hall had been translated from the sombreness of oak to the lightness of enamelled white. Artist plasterers had moulded the lovely Jacobean ceiling, artist stainers had designed and made the great painted windows through which the brightest sea-sunlight was filtered; and when the whole company of three hundred was seated at the tables it seemed not much more than half full, since more than half as many again could find places there without the least crowding. There, amid the strains of gay music and the hum of conversation and the subdued clatter of silver and china and the low throb of the engines, the gay company takes its first meal on the *Titanic*. And as our traveller sits there solitary, he remembers that this is not all, that in another great saloon further off another three hundred passengers of the second class are also at lunch, and that on the floor below him another seven hundred of the third class, and in various other places near a thousand of the crew are also having their meal. All a little oppressive to read about perhaps, but wonderful to contrive and arrange. It is what everyone is thinking and talking about who sits at those luxurious tables, loaded not with seafare, but with dainty and perishable provisions for which half of the countries of the world have been laid under tribute.

The music flows on and the smooth service accomplishes itself; Honour and Glory, high up under the wrought-iron dome of the staircase, are crowning another hour of Time; and our traveller comes up into the fresh air again in order to assure himself that he is really at sea. The electric lift whisks him up four storeys to the deck again; there all around him are the blue-gray waters of

13. A plan of the inside of the *Titanic*.

the Channel surging in a white commotion past the towering sides of the ship, spurned by the tremendous rush and momentum of these fifty thousand tons through the sea. This time our traveller stops short of the boat deck, and begins to explore the far vaster B deck which, sheltered throughout its great length by the boat deck above, and free from all impediments, extends like a vast white roadway on either side of the central deck. Here the busy deck stewards are arranging chairs in the places that will be occupied by them throughout the voyage. Here, as on the parade of a fashionable park, people are taking their walks in the afternoon sunshine.

From the staircase forward the deck houses are devoted to apartments which are still by force of habit called cabins, but which have nothing in fact to distinguish them from the most luxurious habitations ashore, except that no dust ever enters them and that the air is always fresh from the open spaces of the sea.

14. B51, one of *Titanic's* most opulent first class cabins. It was painted white and had a view to the boat deck.

They are not for the solitary traveller; but our friend perhaps is curious and peeps in through an uncurtained window. There is a complete habitation with bedrooms, sitting room, bathroom and service room complete. They breathe an atmosphere of more than mechanical luxury, more than material pleasures. Twin bedsteads, perfect examples of Empire or Louis Seize, symbolise the romance to which the most extravagant luxury in the world is but a minister. Instead of ports there are windows — windows that look straight out on to the blue sea, as might the windows of a castle on a cliff. Instead of stoves or radiators there are open grates, where fires of sea-coal are burning brightly. Every suite is in a different style, and each and all are designed and furnished by artists; and the love and repose of millionaires can be celebrated in surroundings of Adam or Heppelwhite, or Louis Quatorze or the empire, according to their tastes. And for the hire of each of these theatres the millionaire must pay some two hundred guineas a day, with the privilege of being quite alone, cut off from the common herd who are only paying perhaps five-and-twenty pounds a day, and with the privilege, if he chooses, of seeing nothing at all that has to do with a ship, not even the sea.

For there is one thing that the designers of this sea palace seem to have forgotten and seem to be a little ashamed of — and that is the sea itself. There it lies, an eternal prospect beyond these curtained windows, by far the most lovely and wonderful thing visible; but it seems to be forgotten there. True, there is a smoke room at the after extremity of the deck below this, whose windows look out into a great verandah sheeted in with glass from which you cannot help looking upon the sea. But in order to counteract as much as possible that austere and lovely reminder of where we are, trelliswork has been raised within the glass, and great rose trees spread and wander all over it, reminding you by their crimson blossoms of the earth and the land, and the scented shelter of gardens that are far from the boisterous stress of the sea. No spray ever drifts at these heights, no froth or spume can ever in the wildest storms beat upon this verandah. Here, too, as almost everywhere else on this ship, you can, if you will, forget the sea.

15. The verandah café.

16. A first class bedroom on board *Titanic*.

3

Afternoon, Thursday 11 April: Port of Cherbourg

The first afternoon at sea seems long; every face is strange, and it seems as though in so vast a crowd none will ever become familiar, although one of the miracles of sea life is the way in which the blurred crowd resolves itself into individual units, each of which has its character and significance. And if we are really to know and understand and not merely to hear with our ears the tale of what happened to the greatest ship in the world, we must first prepare and soak our minds in her atmosphere, and take in imagination that very voyage which began so happily on this April day. At the end of the afternoon came the coast of France, and Cherbourg — a sunset memory of a long breakwater, a distant cliff crowned with a white building, a fussing of tugs and hasty transference of passengers and mails; and finally the lighthouse showing a golden star against the sunset, when the great ship's head was turned to the red west, and the muffled and murmuring song of the engines was taken up again. Perhaps our traveller, bent upon more discoveries, dined that night not in the saloon, but in the restaurant, and, following the illuminated electric signs that pointed the way along the numerous streets and

17. *Titanic* arrived at Cherboug at dusk, to be met by the tenders *Traffic* and *Nomadic*. Her portholes ablaze with light, she was an awesome sight in the outer roads of the French port.

18. Second class deck of *Titanic*.

roads of the ship, found his way aft to the Cafe Restaurant; where instead of stewards were French waiters and a *maître d'hotel* from Paris, and all the perfection of that perfect and expensive service which condescends to give you a meal for something under a five pound note; where, surrounded by Louis Seize panelling of fawn-coloured walnut, you may on this April evening eat your plovers' egg and strawberries, and drink your 1900 Clicquot, and that in perfect oblivion of the surrounding sea. Afterwards, perhaps, a stroll on the deck amid groups of people, not swathed in peajackets or oilskins, but attired as though for the opera; and all the time, in an atmosphere golden with light, and musical with low-talking voices and the yearning strains of a waltz, driving five-and-twenty miles an hour westward, with the black night and the sea all about us. And then to bed, not in a bunk in a cabin but in a bedstead in a quiet room with a telephone through which to speak to anyone of two thousand people, and a message handed in before you go to sleep that someone wrote in New York since you rose from the dinner-table.

The next morning the scene at Cherbourg was repeated, with the fair green shores of Cork Harbour instead of the cliffs of France for its setting; and then quietly, without fuss, in the early afternoon of Thursday, out round the green point, beyond the headland, and the great ship has steadies on her course and on the long sea road at last. How worn it is! How seamed and furrowed and printed with the tracklines of journeys innumerable; how changing, and yet how unchanged — the road that leads to Archangel or Sicily, to Ceylon or to the frozen Pole; the old road that leads to the ruined gateways of Phoenicia, of Venice, of Tyre; the new road that leads to new lives and new lands; the dustless road, the long road that all must travel who in body or in spirit would really discover a new world. And travel on it as you may for tens of thousands of miles, you come back to it always with the same sense of expectation, never wholly disappointed; and always with the same certainty that you will find at the turn or corner of the road, either some new thing or the renewal of something old.

There is no human experience in which the phenomena of small varieties within one large monotony are so clearly exemplified as in a sea voyage. The dreary beginnings of docks, of baggage, and soiled harbour water; the quite hopeless confusion of strange faces — faces entirely collective, comprising of a mere crowd; the busy highway of the Channel, sunlit or dim with mist or rain, or lightened and bright at night like the main street of a city; the last outpost, the Lizard, with its high gray cliffs, green-roofed, with tiny homesteads perched on the ridge; or Ushant, that tall monitory tower upstanding on the melancholy misty flats; or the solitary Fastnet, lonely, ultimate and watching — these form the familiar overture to the subsequent isolation and vacancy of the long road itself. There are the same day and night of disturbance, the vacant places at table, the prone figures, swathed and motionless in deck-chairs, the morning of brilliant sunshine, when the light that streams into the cabins has a vernal strangeness and wonder for town-dimmed eyes; the gradual emergence of new faces and doubtful staggering back of the demoralized to the blessed freshness of the upper air; the tentative formation of groups and experimental alliances, the rapid disintegration of these and re-formation on entirely new lines; and then that miracle of unending interest and wonder, that the faces that were only the blurred material of a crowd begin one by one to emerge from the background and detach themselves from the mass, to take on identity, individuality, character, till what was a crowd of uninteresting, unidentified humanity becomes a collection of individual persons with whom one's destinies for the time are strangely and unaccountably bound up; among whom one may have acquaintances, friends, or perhaps enemies; who for the inside of a week are all one's world of men and women.

There are few alterative agents so powerful and sure in their working as latitude and longitude; and as we slide across new degrees, habit, association, custom, and ideas slip one by one imperceptibly away from us; we come really into a new world, and if we had no hearts and no memories we should soon become different people. But the heart lives its own life, spinning gossamer threads that float away astern across time and space, joining us invisibly to that which made and fashioned us, and to which we hope to return.

4

Morning, Friday 12 April

Wonderful, even for experienced travellers, is that first waking to a day on which there shall be no sight of the shore, and the first of several days of isolation in the world of a ship. There is a quality in the morning sunshine at sea as it streams into the ship and is reflected in the white paint and sparkling water of the bathrooms, and in the breeze that blows cool and pure along the corridors, that is like nothing else. The company on the *Titanic* woke up on Friday morning to begin in earnest their four days of isolated life. Our traveller, who has found out so many things about the ship, has not found out everything yet; and he continues his explorations, with the advantage, perhaps, of a special permit from the Captain or Chief Engineer to explore other quarters of the floating city besides that in which he lives. Let us, with him, try to form some general conception of the internal arrangements of the ship.

The great superstructure of decks amidships which catches the eye so prominently in a picture or photograph, was but, in reality, a small part, although the most luxurious part, of the vessel. Speaking roughly, one might describe it as consisting of three decks, five hundred feet long, devoted almost exclusively to the accommodation of first class passengers, with the exception of the officers' quarters (situated immediately aft of the bridge on the top deck of all), and the second class smoking room and library, at the after end of the superstructure on the third and fourth decks. With these exceptions, in this great four-storied building were situated all the most magnificent and palatial accommodations of the ship. Immediately beneath it, amidships, in the steadiest part of the vessel where any movement would he least felt, was the first class dining saloon, with the pantries and kitchens immediately aft of it. Two decks below it were the third class dining saloons and kitchens; below them again, separated by a heavy steel deck, were the boiler rooms and coal bunkers, resting on the cellular double bottom of the ship. Immediately aft of the boiler rooms came the two engine rooms; the forward and larger one of the two contained the reciprocating engines which drove the twin screws, and the after one the turbine engine for driving the large centre propeller.

Forward and aft of this centre part of the ship, which in reality occupied about two-thirds of her whole length, were two smaller sections, divided (again one speaks roughly) between second class accommodation, stores and cargo in the stern section, and third class berths, crew's quarters and cargo in the bow section. But although the first class accommodation was all amidships, and the second class all aft, that of the third class was scattered about in such blank spaces as could be found for it. Thus most of the berths were forward, immediately behind the fo'c'stle, some were right aft; the dining room was amidships, and the smoke room in the extreme stern, over the rudder; and to enjoy a smoke or game of cards a third class passenger who was berthed forward would have to walk the whole length of the ship and back again, a walk not far short of half a mile. This gives one an idea of how much more the ship resembled a town than a house. A third class passenger did not walk from his bedroom to his parlour; he walked from the

19. A cutaway illustration of the *Titanic* from *L'Illustration* magazine.

house where he lived in the forward part of the ship to the club a quarter of a mile away where he was to meet his friends.

If, thinking of the *Titanic* storming along westward across the Atlantic, you could imagine her to be split in half from bow to stern so that you could look, as one looks at the section of a hive, upon all her manifold life thus suddenly laid bare, you would find in her a microcosm of civilized society. Up on the top are the rulers, surrounded by the rich and the luxurious, enjoying the best of everything; a little way below them their servants and parasites, ministering not so much to their necessities as to their luxuries; lower down still, at the very base and foundation of all, the fierce and terrible labour of the stokeholds, where the black slaves are shovelling and shovelling as though for dear life, endlessly pouring coal into furnaces that devoured it and yet ever demanded a new supply — horrible labour, joyless life; and yet the labour that gives life and movement to the whole ship. Up above are all the beautiful things. The pleasant things; down below are the terrible and necessary things. Up above are the people who rest and enjoy; down below the people who sweat and suffer.

Consider too the whirl of life and multitude of human employments that you would have found had you peered into this section of the ship that we are supposing to have been laid bare. Honour and Glory, let us say, have just crowned ten o'clock in the morning, beneath the great dome of glass and iron that covers the central staircase. Someone has just come down and posted a notice on the board — a piece of wireless news of something that happened in London last night. In one of the sunny bedrooms (for our section lays everything bare) someone is turning over in bed again and telling a maid to shut out the sun. Eighty feet below her the black slaves are working in a fiery pit; ten feet below them is the green sea. A business-like-looking group have just settled down to bridge in the first class smoking room. The sea does not exist for them, nor the ship; the roses that bloom upon the trelliswork by the verandah interest them no more than the pageant of white clouds which they could see if they looked out of the wide windows. Down below the chief steward, attended by his satellites, is visiting the stores and getting from the storekeeper the necessaries for his day's catering. He has plenty to draw from. In those cold chambers behind the engine room are gathered provisions which

20. View of one of *Titanic's* huge propellers, with ship yard workers in the background giving an idea of the scale just before *Titanic* was about to be launched on 31 May 1911.

seem almost inexhaustible for any population; for the imagination does not properly take in the meaning of such items as a hundred thousand pounds of beef, thirty thousand fresh eggs, fifty tons of potatoes, a thousand pounds of tea, twelve hundred quarts of cream. In charge of the chief steward also, to be checked by him at the end of each voyage, are the china and glass, the cutlery and plate of the ship, amounting in all to some ninety thousand pieces. But there he is, quietly at work with the storekeeper; and not far from him, in another room or series of rooms, another official dealing with the thousands upon thousands of pieces of linen for bed and table with which the town is supplied.

Everything is on a monstrous scale. The centre anchor, which it took a team of sixteen great horses to drag on a wooden trolley, weighs over fifteen tons; its cable will hold a dead weight of three

21. View of the stern and rudder of the *Titanic* in drydock.

hundred tons. The very rudder, that mere slender and almost invisible appendage under the counter, is eighty feet high and weighs a hundred tons. The men on the lookout do not climb up the shrouds and ratlines in the old sea fashion; the mast is hollow and contains a stairway; there is a door in it from which they come out to take their place in the crow's nest.

Are you weary of such statistics? They were among the things on which men thought with pride on those sunny April days in the Atlantic. Man can seldom think of himself apart from his environment, and the house and place in which he lives are ever a preoccupation with all men. From the clerk in his little jerrybuilt villa to the king in his castle, what the house is, what it is built of, how it is equipped and adorned, are matters of vital interest. And if that is true of land, where all the webs of life are connected and intercrossed, how much more must it be true when a man sets his house afloat upon the sea; detaches it from all other houses and from the world, and literally commits himself to it. This was the greatest sea town that had ever been built; these were the first inhabitants of it; theirs were the first lives that were lived in these lovely rooms; this was one of the greatest companies that had ever been afloat together within the walls of one ship. No wonder they were proud; no wonder they were preoccupied wish the source of their pride.

But things stranger still to the life of the sea are happening in some of the hundreds of cells which our giant section-knife has laid bare. An orchestra is practicing in one of them; in another, someone is catching live trout from a pond; Post Office sorters are busy in another with letters for every quarter of the western world; in a garage, mechanicians are cleaning half a dozen motor cars the rippling tones of a piano sound from a drawing room where people are quietly reading in deep velvet armchairs surrounded by books and hothouse flowers in another division people are diving

22. The swimming pool on board *Titanic*.

and swimming in a great bath in water deep enough to drown a tall man; in another an energetic game of squash racquets is in progress; and in great open spaces, on which it is only surprising that turf is not laid, people by hundreds are sunning themselves and breathing the fresh air, utterly unconscious of all these other activities on which we have been looking. For even here, as elsewhere, half of the world does not know and does not care how the other half lives.

All this magnitude had been designed and adapted for the realization of two chief ends — comfort and stability. We have perhaps heard enough about the arrangements for comfort; but the more vital matter had received no less anxious attention. Practically all of the space below the waterline was occupied by the heaviest things in the ship — the boilers, the engines, the coal bunkers and the cargo. And the arrangement of her bulkheads, those tough steel walls that divide a ship's hull into separate compartments, was such that her designers believed that no possible accident short of an explosion in her boilers could sink her. If she rammed any obstruction head on, her bows might crumple up, but the steel walls stretching across her hull — and there were fifteen of them — would prevent the damage spreading far enough aft to sink her. If her broadside was rammed by another ship, and one or even two of these compartments pierced, even then the rest would be sufficient to hold her up at least for a day or two. These bulkheads were constructed of heavy sheet steel, and extended from the very bottom of the ship to a point well above the waterline. Necessarily there were openings in them in order to make possible communication between the different parts of the ship. These openings were the size of an ordinary doorway and fitted with heavy steel doors — not hinged doors, but panels, sliding closely in watertight grooves on either side of the opening. There were several ways of closing them; but once closed they offered a resistance as solid as that of the bulkheads.

The method of opening and closing them was one of the many marvels of modern engineering. The heavy steel doors were held up above the openings by a series of friction clutches. Upon the bridge were switches connected with powerful electro-magnets at the side of the bulkhead openings. The operation of the switches caused each magnet to draw down a heavy weight which instantly released the friction clutches, so that the doors would slide down in a second or two into their places, a gong ringing at the same time to warn anyone who might be passing through to get out of the way. The clutches could also be released by hand. But if for any reason the electric machinery should fail, there was a provision made for closing them automatically in case the ship should be flooded with water. Down in the double bottom of the ship were arranged a series of floats connected with each set of bulkhead doors. In the event of water reaching the compartment below the doors, it would raise the floats, which, in their turn, would release the clutches and drop the doors. These great bulkheads were no new experiment; they had been tried and proved. When the White Star liner *Suevic* was wrecked a few years ago off the Lizard, it was decided to divide the part of her which was floating from the part which was embedded in the rocks and she was cut in two just forward of the main collision bulkhead, and the larger half of her towed into port with no other protection from the sea than this vast steel wall which, nevertheless, easily kept her afloat. And numberless other ships have owed their lives to the resisting power of these steel bulkheads and the quick operation of the sliding doors.

As for the enormous weight that made for the *Titanic's* stability, it was, as I have said, contained chiefly in the boilers, machinery and coal. The coal bunkers were like a lining running round the boilers, not only at the sides of the ship, but also across her whole breadth, thus increasing the solidity of the steel bulkheads; and when it is remembered that her steam was supplied by twenty-nine boilers, each of them the size of a large room, and fired by a hundred and fifty-nine furnaces, the enormous weight of this part of the ship may be dimly realised.

There are two lives lived side by side on such a voyage, the life of the passengers and the life of the ship. From a place high up on the boat deck our traveller can watch the progress of these two lives. The passengers play games or walk about, or sit idly drowsily in deck chairs, with their eyes straying constantly from the unheeded book to the long horizon, or noting the trivial doings of other idlers. The chatter of their voices, the sound of their games, the faint tinkle of music floating up from the music room are eloquent of one of these double lives; there on the bridge is an expression of the other — the bridge in all its spick-and-span sanctities, with the officers of the watch in their trim uniform, the solid quartermaster at the wheel, and his equally solid companion of the watch who dreams his four hours away on the starboard side of the bridge almost as motionless as the bright brass binnacles and standards, and the telegraphs that point unchangeably down to Full Ahead...

The Officer of the watch has a sextant at his eye. One by one the Captain, the Chief, the Second and the Fourth, all come silently up and direct their sextants to the horizon. The quartermaster comes and touches his cap: 'Twelve o'clock, Sir.' There is a silence — a deep sunny silence, broken only by the low tones of the Captain to the Chief: 'What have you got?' says the Captain. 'Thirty,' says the Chief, 'twenty-nine,' says the Third. There is another space of sunny silent sounds; the Captain takes down his sextant. 'Make it eight bells,' he says. Four double strokes resound from the bridge and are echoed from the fo'c'stle head; and the great moment of the day, the moment that means so much, is over. The officers retire with pencils and papers and tables of logarithms; the clock on the staircase is put back, and the day's run posted; from the deck float up the sounds of a waltz and laughing voices; Time and the world flow on with us again.

5

April Ice

For anything that the eye could see the *Titanic*, in all her strength and splendour, was solitary on the ocean. From the highest of her decks nothing could be seen but sea and sky, a vast circle of floor and dome of which, for all her speed of five-and-twenty miles an hour, she remained always the centre. But it was only to the sense of sight that she seemed thus solitary. The North Atlantic, waste of waters though it appears, is really a country crossed and divided by countless tracks as familiar to the seaman as though they were roads marked by trees and milestones. Latitude and longitude, which to a landsman seem mere mathematical abstractions, represent to seamen thousands and thousands of definite points which, in their relation to sun and stars and the measured lapse of time, are each as familiar and as accessible as any spot on a main road is to a landsman. The officer on the bridge may see nothing through his glasses but clouds and waves, yet in his mind's eye he sees not only his own position on the map, which he could fix accurately within a quarter of a mile, but the movements of dozens of other ships coming or going along the great highways. Each ship takes its own road, but it is a road that passes through a certain known territory; the great liners all know each other's movements and where or when they are likely to meet. Many of such meetings are invisible; it is called a meeting at sea if ships pass twenty or thirty miles away from each other and far out of sight.

For there are other senses besides that of sight which now pierce the darkness and span the waste distances of the ocean. It is no voiceless solitude through which the *Titanic* goes on her way. It is full of whispers, summonses, questions, narratives; full of information to the listening ear. High up on the boat deck the little white house to which the wires straggle down from the looped threads between the mastheads is full of the voices of invisible ships that are coming and going beyond the horizon. The wireless impulse is too delicate to be used to actuate a needle like that of the ordinary telegraph; a little voice is given to it, and with this it speaks to the operator who sits with the telephone cap strapped over his ears; a whining, buzzing voice, speaking not in words but in rhythms, corresponding to the dots and dashes made on paper, out of which a whole alphabet has been evolved. And the wireless is the greatest gossip in the world. It repeats everything it hears; it tells the listener everyone else's business. It speaks to him of the affairs of other people as well as his own. It is an ever present eavesdropper, and tells you what other people are saying to one another in exactly the same voice in which they speak to you. When it is sending your messages it shouts, splitting the air with crackling flashes of forked blue fire; but when it has anything to say to you it whispers in your ear in whining, insinuating confidence. And you must listen attentively and with a mind concentrated on your own business if you are to receive from it what concerns you, and reject what does not; for it is not always the loudest whisper that is the most important. The messages come from near and far, now like the rasp of a file in your ear, and now in a thread of sound as fine as the whine of a mosquito and if the mosquito voice is the one that is speaking to you from far away, you may often be interrupted by the loud and empty buzzing of one nearer neighbour speaking to another and loudly interrupting the message which concerns you.

Listening to these voices in the Marconi room of the *Titanic,* and controlling her articulation and hearing, were two young men, little more than boys, but boys of a rare quality, children of the golden age of electricity. Educated in an abstruse and delicate science, and loving the sea for its largeness and adventure, they had come — Phillips at the age of twenty-six, and Bride in the ripe maturity of twenty-one to wield for the *Titanic* the electric forces of the ether, and to direct her utterance and hearing on the ocean. And as they sat there that Friday and Saturday they must have heard, as was their usual routine, all the whispers of the ships for two hundred miles round them, their trained faculties almost automatically rejecting the unessential, receiving and attending to the essential. They heard talk of many things, talk in fragments and in the strange rhythmic language that they had come to know like a mother tongue; talk of cargoes, talk of money and business, of transactions involving thousands of pounds; trivial talk of the emotions, greetings and good wishes exchanged on the high seas; endless figures of latitude and longitude — for a ship is an eternal egoist and begins all her communications by an announcement of Who she is and Where she is. Ships are chiefly interested in weather and cargo, and their wireless talk on their own account is constantly of these things; but most often of the weather. One ship may be pursuing her way under a calm sky and in smooth waters, while two hundred miles away a neighbour may be in the middle of a storm; and so the ships talk to one another of the weather, and combine their forces against it, and, by altering course a little, or rushing ahead, or hanging back, cheat and dodge those malignant forces which are ever pursuing them.

But in these April days there was nothing much to be said about the weather. The winds and the storms were quiet here; they were busy perhaps up in Labrador or furiously raging about Cape Horn, but they had deserted for the time the North Atlantic, and all the ships ploughed steadily on in sunshine and smooth seas. Here and there, however, a whisper came to Phillips or Bride about something which, though not exactly weather, was as deeply interesting to the journeying ships — ice. Just a whisper, nothing more, listened to up there in the sunny Marconi room, recorded, dealt with, and forgotten. 'I have just come through bad field-ice,' whispers one ship; 'April ice very far south,' says another; and Phillips taps out his 'O.K., O.M.,' which is a kind of cockney Marconi for 'All right, old man.' And many other messages come and go, of money and cargoes, and crops and the making of laws; but just now and then a pin-prick of reminder between all these other topics comes the word — ICE.

23. The *Titanic* steamed into an iceberg, but the ice field it was part of covered hundreds of square miles. Passengers view the icefield from an unknown ship.

April ice and April weed are two of the most lovely products of the North Atlantic, but they are strangely opposite in their bearings on human destiny. The lovely golden April weed that is gathered all round the west coast of Ireland, and is burnt for indigo, keeps a whole peasant population in food and clothing for the rest of the year; the April ice, which comes drifting down on the Arctic current from the glacier slopes of Labrador or the plateau of North Greenland, keeps the seafaring population of the North Atlantic in doubt and anxiety throughout the spring and summer. Lovely indeed are some of these icebergs that glitter in the sun like fairy islands or the pinnacles of Valhalla; and dreamy and gentle is their drifting movement as they come down on the current by Newfoundland and round Cape Race, where, meeting the east-going Gulf Stream, they are gradually melted and lost in the waters of the Atlantic. Northward in the drift are often field ice and vast floes; the great detached bergs sail farther south into the steamship tracks, and are what are most carefully looked for. This April there was abundance of evidence that the field ice had come farther south than usual. The *Empress of Britain,* which passed the *Titanic* on Friday, reported an immense quantity of floating ice in the neighbourhood of Cape Race. When she arrived in Liverpool it transpired that, when three days out from Halifax, Nova Scotia, she encountered an ice field, a hundred miles in extent, with enormous bergs which appeared to be joined to the ice field, forming an immense white line, broken with peaks and pinnacles on the horizon. The *Carmania* and the *Nicaragua,* which were going westward ahead of the *Titanic,* had both become entangled in ice, and the *Nicaragua* had sustained considerable damage. And day-by-day, almost hour-by-hour, news was coming in from other ships commenting on the unusual extent southward of the ice field, and on the unusual number of icebergs which they had encountered. No doubt many of the passengers on the *Titanic* were hoping that they would meet with some; it is one of the chief interests of the North Atlantic voyage in the spring and summer; and nothing is more lovely in the bright sunshine of day than the sight of one of these giant islands, with its mountain peaks sparkling in the sun, and blue waves breaking on its crystal shores; nothing more impressive than the thought, as one looks at it, that high as its glittering towers and pinnacles may soar towards heaven there is eight times as great a depth of ice extending downwards into the dark sea. It is only at night, or when the waters are covered with a thick fog produced by the contact of the ice with the warmer water, that navigating officers, peering forward into the mist, know how dreadful may be the presence of one of these sheeted monsters, the ghostly highwaymen of the sea.

6

The Passengers

Information like this, however, only concerned the little group of executive officers who took their turns in tramping up and down the white gratings of the bridge. It was all part of their routine; it was what they expected to hear at this time of the year and in this part of the ocean; there was nothing specially interesting to them in the gossip of the wireless voices. Whatever they heard, we may be sure they did not talk about it to the passengers. For there is one paramount rule observed by the officers of passenger liners — and that is to make everything as pleasant as possible for the passengers. If there is any danger, they are the last to hear of it; if anything unpleasant happens on board, such as an accident or a death, knowledge of it is kept from as many of them as possible. Whatever may be happening, short of an apparent and obvious extremity, it is the duty of the ship's company to help the passenger to believe that he lives and moves and has his being in a kind of Paradise, at the doors of which there are no lurking dangers and in which happiness and pleasure are the first duties of every inhabitant.

And who were the people who composed the population of this journeying town? Subsequent events made their names known to us — vast lists of names filling columns of the newspapers; but to the majority they are names and nothing else. Hardly anyone living knew more than a dozen of them personally; and try as we may it is very hard to see them, as their fellow voyagers must have seen them, as individual human beings with recognizable faces and characters of their own. Of the three hundred odd first class passengers the majority were Americans — rich and prosperous people, engaged for the most part in the simple occupation of buying things as cheaply as possible, selling them as dearly as possible, and trying to find some agreeable way of spending the difference on themselves. Of the three hundred odd second class passengers probably the majority were English, many of them of the minor professional classes and many going either to visit friends or to take up situations in the western world. But the thousand odd steerage passengers represented a kind of Babel of nationalities, all the world in little, united by nothing except poverty and the fact that they were in a transition stage of their existence, leaving behind them for the most part a life of failure and hopelessness, and looking forward to a new life of success and hope: Jews, Christians, and Mohammedans, missionaries and heathen, Russians, Poles, Greeks, Roumanians, Germans, Italians, Chinese, Finns, Spaniards, English, and French — with a strong contingent of Irish, the inevitable link in that melancholy chain of emigration that has united Ireland and America since the Famine. But there were other differences, besides those of their condition and geographical distribution on the ship, that divided its inhabitants. For the first class passengers the world was a very small place, about which many of them were accustomed to hurry in an important way in the process of spending and getting their money, taking an Atlantic liner as humbler people take a tramcar, without giving much thought to it or laying elaborate plans, running backwards and forwards across the Atlantic and its dangers as children run across the road in front of a motor car. They were going to America this week; they would probably come back next week or the week after. They were the people for whom the *Titanic* had specially been designed; it was for them that all the luxuries had been contrived, so that in their runnings backwards and forwards they should not find the long days tedious or themselves divorced from the kind of accompaniments to life which they had come to regard as necessities.

But for the people in the steerage this was no hurrying trip between one business office and another; no hasty holiday arranged to sandwich ten thousand miles of ozone as a refresher between two business engagements. This westward progress was for them part of the drift of their lives; loosening them from their native soil to scatter and distribute them over the New World, in the hope that in fresher soil and less crowded conditions they would strike new roots and begin a new life. The road they travelled was for most of them a road to be travelled once only, a road they knew they would never retrace. For them almost exclusively was reserved that strange sense of looking down over the stern of the ship into the boiling commotion of the churned-up waters, the maelstrom of snow under the counter merging into the pale green highway that lay straight behind them to the horizon, and of knowing that it was a road that divided them from home, a road that grew a mile longer with every three minutes of their storming progress. Other ships would follow on the road; other ships would turn and come again, and drive their way straight back over the white foam to where, with a sudden plunging and turning of screws in the green harbour water of home, the road had begun. But they who looked back from the steerage quarters of the *Titanic* would not return and they, alone of all the passengers on the ship, knew it.

And that is all we can know or imagine about them; but it is probably more than most of the fortunate ones on the snowy upper decks cared to know or imagine. Up there also there were distinctions; some of the travellers there, for example, were so rich that they were conspicuous for riches, even in a population like this — and I imagine that the standard of wealth is higher in the first class population of an Atlantic liner than in any other group of people in the world. There were four men there who represented between them the possession of some seventy millions of money — John Jacob Astor, Isidore Straus, George D. Widener, and Benjamin Guggenheim their names; and it was said that there were twenty who represented a fortune of a hundred millions between them — an interesting, though not an important, fact. But there were people there conspicuous for other things than their wealth. There was William T. Stead who, without any wealth at all, had in some respects changed the thought and social destinies of England; there was Francis Millet, a painter who had attained to eminence in America and who had recently been head of the American Academy in Rome, there was an eminent motorist, an eminent master of hounds, an eminent baseball player, an eminent poloist; and there was Major Archibald Butt, the satellite and right-hand man of Presidents, who had had a typical American career as newspaper correspondent, secretary, soldier, diplomatist, aide-de-camp, and novelist. There was Mr Ismay, the most important man on the ship, for as head of the White Star Line he was practically her owner. He was accompanying her on her maiden voyage with no other object than to find out wherein she was defective, so that her younger sister might excel her. He

24. George Widener (first class passenger), who was lost in the sinking with his son.

25. Isidore Straus, owner of the famous New York department store Macys, who was lost with his wife Ida who refused to enter a lifeboat.

26. The millionaire John Astor who went down with the *Titanic* not before putting his pregnant wife, Madeleine Astor, in lifeboat 4.

27. Bruce Ismay (first class passenger, lifeboat C).

may be said to have accomplished his purpose; and of all the people who took this voyage he is probably the only one who succeeded in what he set out to do. There was Mr Andrews, one of the designers of the *Titanic*, who had come to enjoy the triumph of his giant child; and there were several others also, denizens of that great forest of iron in Belfast Lough, who had seen her and known her when she was a cathedral building within a scaffolding, the most solid and immovable thing in their world. These, the friends and companions of her infancy, had come too, we may suppose, to admire her in her moment of success, as the nurses and humble attendants of some beautiful girl will watch in a body her departure for the triumphs of her first ball.

Of all this throng I had personal knowledge of only two; and yet the two happened to be extremely typical. I knew John Jacob Astor a few years ago in New York, when he sometimes seemed like a polite skeleton in his own gay house; an able but superficially unprepossessing man, so rich that it was almost impossible to know accurately anything about him — a man, I should say, to whom money had been nothing but a handicap from his earliest days. He was typical of this company because he was so conspicuous and so unknown; for when a man has thirty millions of money the world hears about his doings and possessions endlessly, but knows little of the man himself. It is enough to say that there were good things and bad things credited to his account, of which the good were much more unlikely and surprising than the bad.

The other man — and how different! — was Christopher Head. He was typical too, typical of that almost anonymous world that keeps the name of England liked and respected everywhere. I said that he was typical because these few conspicuous names that I have mentioned represent only one narrow class of mankind;

among the unnamed and the unknown you may be sure, if you have any wide experience of collective humanity, that virtues and qualities far more striking and far more admirable were included. Christopher Head was mild and unassuming, and one of the most attractive of men, for wherever he went he left a sense of serenity and security; and he walked through life with a keen, observant intelligence. Outside Lloyd's, of which great corporation he was a member, his interests were chiefly artistic, and he used his interest and knowledge in the best possible way for the public good when he was Mayor of Chelsea, and made his influence felt by imparting some quite new and much-needed ideals into that civic office... But two known faces do not make a crowd familiar and nothing will bring most of us any nearer to the knowledge of these voyagers than will the knowledge of what happened to them.

One thing we do know — a small thing and yet illuminating to our picture. There were many young people on board, many newly married, and some, we may be sure, for whom the voyage represented the gateway to romance; for no Atlantic liner ever sailed with a full complement and set down all its passengers in the emotional state in which it took them up. The sea is a great matchmaker and in those long monotonous hours of solitude many flowers of the heart blossom and many minds and characters strike out towards each other in new and undreamed-of sympathy.

Of this we may be as sure as of the existence of the ship: that there were onboard the *Titanic* people watching the slip of moon setting early on those April nights for whom time and the world were quite arrested in their course, and for whom the whole ship and her teeming activities were, but frame and setting for the perfect moment of their lives; for whom the thronging multitudes of their fellow passengers were but a blurred background against which the colour of their joy stood sharp and clear. The fields of foam-flecked blue, sunlit or cloud-shadowed by day; the starlight on the waters; the slow and scarcely perceptible swinging of the ship's rail against the violet and spangled sky; the low murmur of voices, the liquid notes of violins, the trampling tune of the engines — to how many others have not these been the properties of a magic world; for how many others, as long as men continue to go in ships upon the sea, will they not be the symbols of a joy that is as old as time, and that is found to be new by every generation! For this also is one of the gifts of the sea, and one of the territories through which the long road passes.

7

Sunday at Sea

Sunday came, with nothing to mark it except the morning service in the saloon — a function that by reason of its novelty, attracts some people at sea who do not associate it with the shore. One thing, however, fire or boat muster, which usually marks a Sunday at sea, and gives it a little variety, did not for some reason take place. It is one of the few variants of the monotony of ship-board life, where anything in the nature of a spectacle is welcomed; and most travellers are familiar with the stir called by the sudden hoarse blast of the foghorn and the subsequent patter of feet and appearance from below all kinds of people whose existence the passenger had hardly suspected. Stewards, sailors, firemen, engineers, nurses, bakers, butchers, cooks, florists, barbers, carpenters, and stewardesses, ranged in two immense lines along the boat deck, answer to their names and are told off, according to their numbers, to take charge of certain boats. This muster did not take place on the *Titanic*; if it had it would have revealed to any observant passenger the fact that the whole crew of nine hundred would have occupied all the available accommodation in the boats hanging on the davits and left no room for any passengers. For the men who designed and built the *Titanic*, who knew the tremendous strength of the girders and cantilevers and bulkheads which took the thrust and pull of every strain that she might undergo, had thought of boats rather as a superfluity, dating from the days when ships were vulnerable, when they sprang leaks and might sink in the high seas. In their pride they had said 'the *Titanic* cannot spring a leak.' So there was no boat muster, and the routine occupations of Sunday went on unvaried and undisturbed. Only in the Marconi room was the monotony varied, for something had gone wrong with the delicate electrical apparatus, and the wireless voice was silent; and throughout the morning and afternoon, for seven hours, Phillips and Bride were hard at work testing and searching for the little fault that had cut them off from the world of voices. And at last they found it, and the whining and buzzing began again. But it told them nothing new; only the same story, whispered this time from the *Californian* — the story of ice.

The day wore on, the dusk fell, lights one by one sprang up and shone within the ship; the young moon rose in a cloudless sky spangled with stars. People remarked on the loveliness of the night as they went to dress for dinner, but they remarked also on its coldness. There was an unusual chill in the air, and lightly clad people were glad to draw in to the big fireplaces in smoke room or drawing room or library, and to keep within the comfort of the warm and lamp lit rooms. The cold was easily accounted for; it was the ice season, and the airs that were blowing down from the north-west carried with them a breath from the ice fields. It was so cold that the decks were pretty well deserted, and the usual evening concert, instead of being held on the open deck, was held in the warmth, under cover. And gradually people drifted away to bed, leaving only a few late birds sitting up reading in the library or playing cards in the smoking rooms, or following a restaurant dinner party by quiet conversation in the flower-decked lounge.

The ship had settled down for the night; half of her company were peacefully asleep in bed, and many lying down waiting for sleep to come, when something happened. What that something was depended upon what part of the ship you were in. The first thing to attract the attention of most of the first class passengers was a negative thing — the cessation of that trembling, continuous rhythm which had been the undercurrent of all their waking sensations since the ship left Queenstown. The engines stopped. Some wondered, and put their heads out of their stateroom doors, or even threw a wrap about them and went out into the corridors to see what had happened, while others turned over to bed and composed themselves to sleep, deciding to wait until the morning to hear what was the cause of the delay.

Lower down in the ship they heard a little more. The sudden harsh clash of the engine room telegraph bells would startle those who were near enough to hear it, especially as it was followed almost immediately afterwards by the simultaneous ringing all through the lower part of the ship of the gongs that gave warning of the closing of the watertight doors. After the engines stopped there was a moment of stillness; and then the vibration began again, more insistently this time, with a certain jumping movement which to the experienced ear meant that the engines were being sent full speed astern; and then they stopped again, and again there was stillness.

Here and there in the long corridors amidships a door opened and some one thrust a head out, asking what was the matter; here and there a man in pyjamas and a dressing gown came out of his cabin and climbed up the deserted staircase to have a look at what was going on; people sitting in the lighted saloons and smoke rooms looked at one another and said: 'What was that?' gave or received some explanation, and resumed their occupations. A man in his dressing gown came into one of the smoking rooms where a party was seated at cards, with a few yawning bystanders looking on before they turned in. The newcomer wanted to know what was the matter, whether they had noticed anything? They had felt a slight jar, they said, and had seen an iceberg going by past the windows; probably the ship had grazed it, but no damage had been done. And they resumed their game of bridge. The man in the dressing gown left the smoke room, and never saw any of the players again. So little excitement was there in this part of the ship that the man in the dressing gown (his name was Mr Beesley, an English schoolmaster, one of the few who emerges from the crowd with an intact individuality) went back to his cabin and lay down on his bed with a book, waiting for the ship to start again. But the unnatural stillness, the uncanny peace even of this great peaceful ship, must have got a little upon his nerves; and when he heard people moving about in the corridors, he got up again, and found that several people whom the stillness had wakened from their sleep were wandering about inquiring what had happened.

But that was all. The half-hour which followed the stoppage of the ship was a comparatively quiet half-hour, in which a few people came out of their cabins indeed, and collected together in the corridors and staircases gossiping, speculating and asking questions as to what could have happened; but it was not a time of anxiety, or anything like it. Nothing could be safer on this quiet Sunday night than the great ship, warmed and lighted everywhere, with her thick carpets and padded armchairs and cushioned recesses; and if anything could have added to the sense of peace and stability, it was that her driving motion had ceased, and that she lay solid and motionless like a rock in the sea, the still water scarcely lapping against her sides. And those of her people who had thought it worth while to get out of bed stood about in little knots, and asked foolish questions, and gave foolish answers in the familiar manner of passengers on shipboard when the slightest incident occurs to vary the regular and monotonous routine.

28. View from *Carpathia* of the iceberg which sank the *Titanic*.

8

'Close the Water-Tight Doors':
11.40pm Sunday 14 April

This was one phase of that first half-hour. Up on the high bridge, isolated from all the indoor life of the passengers, there was another phase. The watches had been relieved at ten o'clock, when the ship had settled down for the quietest and least eventful period of the whole twenty-four hours. The First Officer, Mr Murdoch, was in command of the bridge, and with him was Mr Boxhall, the Fourth Officer, and the usual lookout staff. The moon had set, and the night was very cold, clear and starry, except where here and there a slight haze hung on the surface of the water. Captain Smith, to whom the night of the sea was like day, and to whom all the invisible tracks and roads of the Atlantic were as familiar as Fleet Street is to a *Daily Telegraph* reporter, had been in the chart room behind the bridge to plot out the course for the night, and afterwards had gone to his room to lie down. Two pairs of sharp eyes were peering forward from the crow's nest, another pair from the nose of the ship on the fo'c'stle head, and at least three pairs from the bridge itself, all staring into the dim night, quartering with busy glances the area of the black sea in front of them where the foremast and its wire shrouds and stays were swinging almost imperceptibly across the starry sky.

29. View of the gangway of *Titanic* shows First Officer Murdoch and Second Officer Lightoller looking out from the ship.

30. The captain of the *Titanic*, Edward Smith.

At twenty minutes to twelve the silence of the night was broken by three sharp strokes on the gong sounding from the crow's nest — a signal for something right ahead; while almost simultaneously came a voice through the telephone from the lookout announcing the presence of ice. There was a kind of haze in front of the ship the colour of the sea, but nothing could be distinguished from the bridge. Mr Murdoch's hand was on the telegraph immediately, and his voice rapped out the order to the quartermaster to starboard the helm. The wheel spun round, the answering click came up from the startled engine room, but before anything else could happen there was a slight shock, and a splintering sound from the bows of the ship as she crashed into yielding ice. That was followed by a rubbing, jarring, grinding sensation along her starboard bilge, and a peak of dark coloured ice glided past close alongside.

As the engines stopped in obedience to the telegraph Mr Murdoch turned the switches that closed the watertight doors. Captain Smith came running out of the chart room. 'What is it?' he asked. 'We have struck ice, Sir.' 'Close the water-tight doors.' 'It is already done, Sir.' Then the Captain took command. He at once sent a message to the carpenter to sound the ship and come and report; the quartermaster went away with the message, and set the carpenter to work. Captain Smith now gave a glance at the commutator, a dial which shows to what extent the ship is off the perpendicular, and noticed that she carried a 5° list to starboard. Coolly following a routine as exact as that which he would have observed had he been conning the ship into dock, he gave a number of orders in rapid succession, after first consulting with the Chief Engineer. Then, having given instructions that the whole of the available engine power was to be turned to pumping the ship, he hurried aft along the boat deck to the Marconi room. Phillips was sitting at his key, toiling through routine business; Bride, who had just

31. Longitudinal section of the *Titanic* showing the layout of first, second and third class accomadation, her bulkheads and compartments from a 1912 newspaper. The arrow indicates where it was thought in 1912, the iceberg had struck, the heavy black line indicates the damaged area caused by the collision.

got up to relieve him, was sleepily making preparations to take his place. The Captain put his head in at the door.

'We have struck an iceberg,' he said, 'and I am having an inspection made to tell what it has done for us. Better get ready to send out a call for assistance, but don't send it until I tell you.'

He hurried away again; in a few minutes he put his head in at the door again; 'Send that call for assistance,' he said.

'What call shall I send?' asked Phillips.

'The regulation international call for help, just that,' said the Captain, and was gone again.

But in five minutes he came back into the wireless room, this time apparently not in such a hurry. 'What call are you sending?' he asked; and when Phillips told him 'C.Q.D.,' the highly technical and efficient Bride suggested, laughingly, that he should send 'S.O.S.,' the new international call for assistance which has superseded the C.Q.D. 'It is the new call,' said Bride, 'and it may be your last chance to send it!' And they all three laughed, and then for a moment chatted about what had happened, while Phillips tapped out the three longs, three shorts, and three longs which instantaneously sent a message of appeal flashing out far and wide into the dark night. The Captain, who did not seem seriously worried or concerned, told them that the ship had been struck amidships or a little aft of that.

Whatever may have been happening down below, everything up here was quiet and matter-of-fact. It was a disaster, of course, but everything was working well, everything had been done; the electric switches for operating the bulkhead doors had been used promptly, and had worked beautifully; the powerful wireless plant was talking to the ocean, and in a few hours there would be some other ship alongside of them. It was rough luck, to be sure; they had not thought they would so soon have a chance of proving that the *Titanic* was unsinkable.

32. Sunday 14 April 1912, 11.45pm *Titanic* strikes an iceberg with its starboard bow, 12 feet aft. This illustration is the first of a series of 6 sketches drawn on board *Carpathia* by Lewis Skidmore a young art teacher, and *Carpathia* pasenger, based on conversations he had had with Jack Thayer (first class passenger, lifeboat B) following the rescue.

9

Muster on the Boat Deck

We must now visit in imagination some other parts of the ship, parts isolated from the bridge and the spacious temple of luxury amidships, and try to understand how the events of this half hour appeared to the denizens of the lower quarters of the ship. The impact that had been scarcely noticed in the first class quarters had had much more effect down below, and especially forward, where some of the third class passengers and some of the crew were berthed. A ripping, grinding crash startled all but the heaviest sleepers here into wakefulness; but it was over so soon and was succeeded by so peaceful a silence that no doubt any momentary panic it might have caused was soon allayed. One of the firemen describing it said: 'I was awakened by a noise, and between sleeping and waking I thought I was dreaming that I was on a train that had run off the lines, and that I was being jolted about.' He jumped out and went on deck, where he saw the scattered ice lying about. 'Oh, we have struck an iceberg,' he said, 'that's nothing; I shall go back and turn in,' and he actually went back to bed and slept for half an hour, until he was turned out to take his station at the boats.

The steerage passengers, who were berthed right aft, heard nothing and knew nothing until the news that an accident had happened began slowly to filter down to them. But there was no one in authority to give them any official news, and for a time they were left to wonder and speculate as they chose. Forward, however, it became almost immediately apparent to certain people that there was something grievously wrong; firemen on their way through the passage along the ship's bottom leading between their quarters and No. 1 stokehold found water coming in, and rapidly turned back. They were met on their way up the staircase by an officer who asked them what they were doing. They told him. 'There's water coming into our place, Sir,' they said; and as he thought they were off duty he did not turn them back.

Mr Andrews, a partner in Harland and Wolff's, and one of the *Titanic*'s designers, had gone quietly down by himself to investigate the damage, and, great as was his belief in the giant he had helped to create, it must have been shaken when he found the water pouring into her at the rate of hundreds of tons a minute. Even his confidence in those mighty steel walls that stretched one behind the other in succession along the whole length of the ship could not have been proof against the knowledge that three or four of them had been pierced by the long rip of the ice-tooth. There was just a chance that she would hold up long enough to allow of relief to arrive in time; but it is certain that from that movement Mr Andrews devoted himself to warning people, and helping to get them away, so far as he could do so without creating a panic.

Most of the passengers, remember, were still asleep during this half hour. One of the most terrible things possible at sea is a panic, and Captain Smith was particularly anxious that no alarm should be given before or unless it was absolutely necessary. He heard what Mr Andrews had to say, and consulted with the engineer, and soon found that the whole of the ship's bottom was being flooded. There were other circumstances calculated to make the most sanguine shipmaster uneasy. Already, within half an hour, the *Titanic* was perceptibly down by the head. She would remain stationary for five minutes and then drop six inches or a foot; remain stationary again, and drop another foot — a circumstance ominous to experienced minds, suggesting that some of the smaller compartments forward were one by one being flooded, and letting the water farther and farther into her hull.

Therefore at about twenty-five minutes past midnight the Captain gave orders for the passengers to be called and mustered on the boat deck. All the ship's crew had by this time been summoned to their various stations; and now through all the carpeted corridors, through the companion-ways and up and down staircases, leading to the steerage cabins, an army of three hundred stewards was hurrying, knocking loudly on doors, and shouting up and down the passages, 'All passengers on deck with

SETTLES BY HEAD · BOATS ORDERED OUT

33. Monday 15 April 1912, 12.05am *Titanic* settles by head, boats ordered out.

lifebelts on!' The summons came to many in their sleep; and to some in the curtained firelight luxury of their deck state rooms it seemed an order so absurd that they scorned it, and actually went back to bed again. These, however, were rare exceptions; for most people there was no mistaking the urgency of the command, even though they were slow to understand the necessity for it. And hurry is a thing easily communicated; seeing some passengers hastening out with nothing over their night clothes but a blanket or a wrapper, others caught the infection, and hurried too; and struggling with lifebelts, clumsily attempting to adjust them over and under a curious assortment of garments, the passengers of the *Titanic* came crowding up on deck, for the first time fully alarmed.

10

'Women & Children First': The Lowering of the Lifeboats

When the people came on deck it was half-past twelve. The first class passengers came pouring up the two main staircases and out on to the boat deck — some of them indignant, many of them curious, some few of them alarmed. They found there everything as usual except that the long deck was not quite level; it tilted downwards a little towards the bow, and there was a slight list towards the starboard side. The stars were shining in the sky and the sea was perfectly smooth, although dotted about it here and there were lumps of dark coloured ice, almost invisible against the background of smooth water. A long line of stewards was forming up beside the boats on either side — those solid white boats, stretching far aft in two long lines that became suddenly invested with practical interest. Officers were shouting orders, seamen were busy clearing up the coils of rope attached to the davit tackles, fitting the iron handles to the winches by which the davits themselves were canted over from the inward position over the deck to the outward position over the ship's side. Almost at the same time a rush of people began from the steerage quarters, swarming up stairways and ladders to reach this high deck hitherto sacred to the first class passengers. At first they were held back by a cordon of stewards, but some broke through and others were allowed through, so that presently a large proportion of the ship's company was crowding about the boat deck and the one immediately below it.

Then the business of clearing, filling, and lowering the boats was begun — business quickly described, but occupying a good deal of time in the transaction. Mr Murdoch the Chief Officer, ordered the crews to the boats; and with some confusion different parties of stewards and sailors disentangled themselves from the throng and stood in their positions by each of the sixteen boats. Every member of the crew, when he signs on for a voyage in a big passenger ship, is given a number denoting which boat's crew he belongs to. If there has been a boat drill, every man knows and remembers his number; if, as in the case of the *Titanic*, there has been no boat drill some of the men remember their numbers and some do not, the result being a certain amount of confusion. But at last a certain number of men were allotted to each boat, and began the business of hoisting them out.

First of all the covers had to be taken off and the heavy masts and sails lifted out of them. Ship's boats appear very small things when one sees a line of them swinging high up on deck; but, as a matter of fact they are extremely heavy, each of them the size of a small sailing yacht. Everything on the *Titanic* having been newly painted, everything was stiff and difficult to move. The lashings of the heavy canvas covers were like wire, and the covers themselves like great boards; the new ropes ran stiffly in the new gear. At last a boat was cleared and the order given, 'Women and children first.' The officers had revolvers in their hands ready to prevent a rush; but there was no rush. There was a certain amount of laughter. No one wanted to be the first to get into the boat and leave the ship.

'Come on,' cried the officers. There was a pause, followed by the brief command, 'Put them in.'

The crew seized the nearest women and pushed or lifted them over the rail into the first boat, which was now hanging over the side level with the deck. But they were very unwilling to go. The boat, which looked big and solid on the deck, now hung dizzily seventy-five feet over the dark water; it seemed a far from attractive prospect to get into it and go out on to the cold sea, especially as everyone was convinced that it was a merely formal precaution which was being taken, and that the people in the boats would merely be rowed off a little way and kept shivering on the cold sea for a time and then brought back to the ship when it was found that the danger was past. For, walking about the deck, people remembered all the things that they had been thinking and saying since first they had seen the *Titanic*; and what was the use of travelling by an unsinkable ship if, at the first alarm of danger, one had to leave her and row out on the icy water? Obviously it was only the old habit of the sea asserting itself, and Captain Smith, who had hitherto been such a favourite, was beginning to be regarded as something of a nuisance with his ridiculous precautions.

The boats swung and swayed in the davits; even the calm sea, now that they looked at it more closely, was seen to be not absolutely like a millpond, but to have a certain movement on its surface which, although utterly helpless to move the huge bulk of the *Titanic*, against whose sides it lapped, as ineffectually as against the walls of a dock, was enough to impart a swinging movement to the small boats. But at last, what with coercion and persuasion, a boat was half filled with women. One of the things they liked least was leaving their husbands; they felt that they

34. The scenes aboard as women were ushered to the lifeboats. In practice, much of the loading was much less orderly than this.

35. The male passengers wish their sweethearts goodbye. Some women chose to remain with their menfolk and take the chance onboard ship.

36. It was 75ft from the boat deck to the calm seas below. Many boats left only part full. Of the 1,000 possible lives that could have been saved, only just over 700 actually survived the sinking.

37. Heart breaking farewells. Romanticised view of the scene on the Boat Deck as husbands and wives were parted from the 1912 account by Logan Marshall.

were being sacrificed needlessly to over-elaborate precautions, and it was hard to leave the men standing comfortably on the firm deck, sheltered and in a flood of warm yellow light, and in the safety of the great solid ship that lay as still as a rock, while they had to go out, half-clad and shivering, on the icy waters.

But the inexorable movements of the crew continued. The pulleys squealed in the sheaves, the new ropes were paid out; and jerking downwards, a foot or two at a time, the first boat dropped down towards the water, past storey after storey of the great structure, past rows and rows of lighted portholes, until at last, by strange unknown regions of the ship's side, where cataracts and waterfalls were rushing into the sea, it rested on the waves. The blocks were unhooked, the heavy ash oars were shipped, and the boat headed away into the darkness. And then, and not till then, those in the boat realized that something was seriously wrong with the *Titanic*. Instead of the trim level appearance which she presented on the picture postcards or photographs, she had an ungraceful slant downwards to the bows — a heavy helpless appearance like some wounded monster that is being overcome by the waters. And even while they looked, they could see that the bow was sinking lower.

After the first boat had got away, there was less difficulty about the others. The order, 'Women and children first,' was rigidly enforced by the officers; but it was necessary to have men in the boats to handle them, and a number of stewards, and many grimy figures of stokers who had mysteriously appeared from below were put into them to man them. Once the tide of people began to set into the boats and away from the ship, there came a certain anxiety to join them and not to be left behind. Here and there indeed there was over-anxiety, which had to be roughly checked. One band of Italians from the steerage, who had good reason to know that something was wrong, tried to rush one of the boats, and had to be kept back by force, an officer firing a couple of shots with his pistol; they desisted, and were hauled back ignominiously by the legs. In their place some of the crew and the passengers who were helping lifted in a number of Italian women limp with fright.

And still everyone was walking about and saying that the ship was unsinkable. There was a certain subdued excitement, natural to those who feel that they are taking part in a rather thrilling adventure which will give them importance in the eyes of people at home when they relate it. There was as yet no call for heroism, because, among the first class passengers certainly, the majority believed that the safest as well as the most comfortable place was the ship. But it was painful for husbands and wives to be separated, and the wives sent out to brave the discomforts of the open boats while the husbands remained on the dry and comfortable ship.

The steerage people knew better and feared more. Life had not taught them, as it had taught some of those first class passengers, that the world was an organization specially designed for their comfort and security; they had not come to believe that the crude and ugly and elementary catastrophes of fate would not attack them. On the contrary, most of them knew destiny as a thing to fear, and made haste to flee from it. Many of them, moreover, had been sleeping low down in the forward part of the ship; they had heard strange noises, had seen water washing about where no water should be, and they were frightened. There was, however, no discrimination between classes in putting the women into the boats. The woman with a tattered shawl over her head, the woman with a sable coat over her nightdress, the woman clasping a baby, and the woman clutching a packet of trinkets had all an equal chance; side by side they were handed on to the harsh and uncomfortable thwarts of the lifeboats; the wife of the millionaire sat cheek by jowl with a dusty stoker and a Russian emigrant, and the spoiled woman of the world found some poor foreigner's baby thrown into her lap as the boat was lowered.

By this time the women and children had all been mustered on the second or A deck; the men were supposed to remain up on the boat deck while the boats were being lowered to the level of the women, where sections of the rail had been cleared away for them to embark more easily; but this rule, like all the other rules, was not rigidly observed. The crew was not trained enough to discipline and coerce the passengers. How could they be? They were trained to serve them, to be obsequious and obliging; it would have been too much to expect that they should suddenly take command and order them about.

There were many minor adventures and even accidents. One woman had both her legs broken in getting into the boat. The mere business of being lowered in a boat through seventy feet of darkness was in itself productive of more than one exciting incident. The falls of the first boat jammed when she was four feet from the water, and she had to be dropped into it with a splash. And there was one very curious incident which happened to the boat in which Mr Beesley, the English schoolmaster already referred to, had been allotted a place as a helper. 'As the boat began to descend,' he said, 'two ladies were pushed hurriedly through the crowd on B deck, and a baby ten months old was passed down after them. Then down we went, the crew shouting out directions to those lowering us. "Level," "Aft," "Stern," "Both together!" until we were some ten feet from the water. Here occurred the only anxious moment we had during the whole of our experience from the time of our leaving the deck to our reaching the *Carpathia*.'

'Immediately below our boat was the exhaust of the condensers, and a huge stream of water was pouring all the time from the ship's side just above the waterline. It was plain that we ought to be smart away from it if we were to escape swamping when we touched the water. We had no officers on board, and no petty officer or member of the crew to take charge, so one of the stokers shouted, "Some one find the pin which releases the boat from the ropes and pull it up!" No one knew where it was. We felt as well as we could on the floor, and along the sides, but found nothing. It was difficult to move among so many people. We had sixty or seventy on board. Down we went, and presently we floated with our ropes still holding us, and the stream of water from the exhaust washing us away from the side of the vessel, while the swell of the sea urged us back against the side again.'

'The result of all these forces was that we were carried parallel to the ship's side, and directly under boat No. 14, which had filled rapidly with men, and was coming down on us in a way that threatened to submerge our boat.'

'"Stop lowering 14," our crew shouted, and the crew of No. 14, now only 20 feet above, cried out the same. The distance to the top, however, was some 70 feet, and the creaking of the pulleys must have deadened all sound to those above, for down she came, 15 feet, 10 feet, 5 feet, and a stoker and I reached up and touched the bottom of the swinging boat above our heads. The next drop would have brought her on our heads. Just before she dropped another stoker sprang to the ropes with his knife open in his hand. "One," I heard him say, and then "Two," as the knife cut through the pulley rope.'

'The next moment the exhaust stream carried us clear, while boat No. 14 dropped into the water, taking the space we had occupied a moment before. Our gunwales were almost touching. We drifted away easily, and when our oars were got out, we headed directly away from the ship.'

But although there was no sense of danger, there were some painful partings on the deck where the women were embarked; for you must think of this scene as going on for at least an hour amid a confusion of people pressing about, trying to find their friends, asking for information, listening to some new rumour, trying to decide whether they should or should not go in the boats, to a constant accompaniment of shouted orders, the roar of escaping steam, the squeal and whine of the ropes and pulleys, and the gay music of the band, which Captain Smith had ordered to play during the embarkation. Every now and then a woman would be forced away from her husband; every now and then a husband, having got into a boat with his wife, would be made to get out of it again. If it was hard for the wives to go, it was harder for the husbands to see them go to such certain discomfort and in such strange company. Colonel Astor, whose young wife was in a delicate state of health, had got into the boat with her to look after her; and no wonder. But he was ordered out again and came at once, no doubt feeling bitterly, poor soul, that he would have given many of his millions to be able to go honourably with her. But he stepped back without a word of remonstrance and gave her goodbye with a cheery message, promising to meet her in New York. And if that happened to him, we may be sure it was happening over and over again in other boats. There, were women who flatly refused to leave their husbands and chose to stay with them and risk whatever fate might be in store for them, although at that time most of the people did not really believe that there was much danger. Yet here and there there were incidents both touching and heroic. When it came to the turn of

Mrs Isidore Straus, the wife of a Jewish millionaire, she took her seat but got back out of the boat when she found her husband was not coming. They were both old people, and on two separate occasions an Englishman who knew her tried to persuade her to get into a boat, but she would not leave her husband. The second time the boat was not full and he went to Mr Straus and said: 'Do go with your wife. Nobody can object to an old gentleman like you going. There is plenty of room in the boat.' The old gentleman thanked him calmly and said: 'I won't go before the other men.' And Mrs Straus got out and, going up to him, said: 'We have been together for forty years and we will not separate now.' And she remained by his side until that happened to them which happened to the rest.

11

'Every Man for Himself'

We must now go back to the Marconi room on the upper deck where, ten minutes after the collision, Captain Smith had left the operators with orders to send out a call for assistance. From this Marconi room we get a strange but vivid aspect of the situation; for Bride, the surviving operator, who afterwards told the story so graphically to the *New York Times*, practically never left the room until he left it to jump into the sea, and his knowledge of what was going on was the vivid, partial knowledge of a man who was closely occupied with his own duties and only knew of other happenings in so far as they affected his own doings. They had been working, you will remember, almost all of that Sunday at locating and replacing a burnt-out terminal, and were both very tired. Phillips was taking the night shift of duty, but he told Bride to go to bed early and get up and relieve him as soon as he had had a little sleep, as Phillips himself was quite worn out with his day's work. Bride went to sleep in the cabin which opened into the operating room.

He slept some time, and when he woke he heard Phillips still at work. He could read the rhythmic buzzing sounds as easily as you or I can read print. He could hear that Phillips was talking to Cape Race, sending dull uninteresting traffic matter; and he was about to sink off to sleep again when he remembered how tired Phillips must be, and decided that he would get up and relieve him for a spell. He never felt the shock, or saw anything, or had any other notification of anything unusual except no doubt the ringing of the telegraph bells and cessation of the beat of the engines. It was a few minutes afterwards that, as we have seen, the Captain put his head in at the door and told them to get ready to send a call, returning ten minutes later to tell them to send it.

The two operators were rather amused than otherwise at having to send out the S.O.S.; it was a pleasant change from relaying traffic matter. 'We said lots of funny things to each other in the next few minutes,' said Bride. Phillips went stolidly on,

38. Wireless operator sending messages. But for the wireless, the *Titanic's* passengers would surely have all been lost, as they could not have survived on the Atlantic in the small lifeboats for long.

firmly hammering out his 'S.O.S., S.O.S.,' sometimes varying it with 'C.Q.D.' for the benefit of such operators as might not be on the alert for the new call. For several minutes there was no reply; then the whining voice at Phillips' ear began to answer. Some one had heard. They had picked up the steamer *Frankfurt*, and they gave her the position and told her that the *Titanic* had struck an iceberg and needed assistance. There was another pause and, in their minds' eye, the wireless men could see the *Frankfurt's* operator miles and miles away across the dark night going along from his cabin and rousing the *Frankfurt's* Captain and giving his message and coming back to the instrument, when again the whining voice began asking for more news.

They were learning facts up here in the Marconi room. They knew that the *Titanic* was taking in water, and they knew that she was sinking by the head; and what they knew they flashed out into the night for the benefit of all who had ears to hear. They knew that there were many ships in their vicinity; but they knew also that hardly any of them carried more than one operator, and that even Marconi operators earning £4 a month must go to bed and sleep sometimes, and that it was a mere chance if their call was heard. But presently the Cunard liner *Carpathia* answered and told them her position, from which it appeared that she was about seventy miles away. The *Carpathia*, which was heading towards the Mediterranean, told them she had altered her course and was heading full steam to their assistance. The *Carpathia's* voice was much fainter than the *Frankfurt's*, from which Phillips assumed that the *Frankfurt* was the nearer ship; but there was a certain lack of promptitude on board the *Frankfurt* which made Phillips impatient. While he was still sending out the call for help, after the *Frankfurt* had answered it, she interrupted him again, asking what was the matter. They told Captain Smith, who said, 'That fellow is a fool,' an opinion which Phillips and Bride not only shared, but which they even found time to communicate to the operator on the *Frankfurt*. By this time the *Olympic* had also answered her twin sister's cry for help, but she was far away, more than three hundred miles; and although she too turned and began to race towards the spot where the *Titanic* was lying so quietly, it was felt that the honours of saving her passengers would go to the *Carpathia*. The foolish *Frankfurt* operator still occasionally interrupted with a question, and he was finally told, with such brusqueness as the wireless is capable of, to keep away from his instrument and not interfere with the serious conversations of the *Titanic* and *Carpathia*.

Then Bride took Phillips's place at the instrument and succeeded in getting a whisper from the *Baltic*, and gradually, over hundreds of miles of ocean, the invisible ether told the ships that their giant sister was in distress. The time passed quickly with these urgent conversations on which so much might depend, and hour-by-hour, and minute-by-minute the water was creeping up the steep sides of the ship. Once the Captain looked in and told them that the engine rooms were taking in water and that the dynamos might not last much longer. That information was also sent to the *Carpathia*, who by this time could tell them that she had turned towards them with every furnace going at full blast, and was hurrying forward at the rate of eighteen knots instead of her usual fifteen. It now became a question how long the storage plant would continue to supply current. Phillips went out on deck and looked round. 'The water was pretty close up to the boat deck. There was a great scramble aft, and how poor Phillip worked through it I don't know. He was a brave man. I learnt to love him that night, and I suddenly

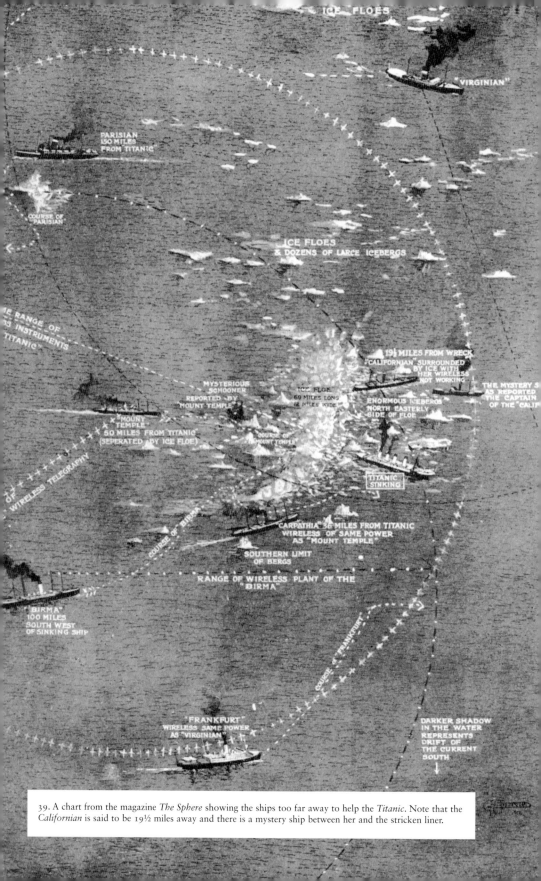

ICE FLOES

"VIRGINIAN"

PARISIAN
150 MILES
FROM TITANIC

COURSE OF
"PARISIAN"

ICE FLOES
& DOZENS OF LARGE ICEBERGS

...E RANGE OF
...S INSTRUMENTS
...TITANIC

19½ MILES FROM WRECK
"CALIFORNIAN" SURROUNDED
BY ICE WITH
HER WIRELESS
NOT WORKING

THE MYSTERY S...
AS REPORTED
THE CAPTAIN
OF THE "CALIF...

MYSTERIOUS
SCHOONER
REPORTED BY
MOUNT TEMPLE

ICE FLOE
60 MILES LONG
14 MILES WIDE

ENORMOUS ICEBERGS
NORTH EASTERLY
SIDE OF FLOE

"MOUNT
TEMPLE
50 MILES FROM TITANIC
(SEPERATED BY ICE FLOE)

COURSE OF
...MOUNT TEMPLE

...OF
...WIRELESS TELEGRAPHY

COURSE OF BIRMA

TITANIC
SINKING

CARPATHIA 58 MILES FROM TITANIC
WIRELESS OF SAME POWER
AS "MOUNT TEMPLE"

SOUTHERN LIMIT
OF BERGS

RANGE OF WIRELESS PLANT OF THE
"BIRMA"

"BIRMA"
100 MILES
SOUTH WEST
OF SINKING SHIP

COURSE OF FRANKFURT

DARKER SHADOW
IN THE WATER
REPRESENTS
DRIFT OF
THE CURRENT
SOUTH

"FRANKFURT"
WIRELESS SAME POWER
AS "VIRGINIAN"

39. A chart from the magazine *The Sphere* showing the ships too far away to help the *Titanic*. Note that the *Californian* is said to be 19½ miles away and there is a mystery ship between her and the stricken liner.

felt for him a great reverence, to see him standing there sticking to his work while everybody else was raging about. While I live I shall never forget the work Phillips did for that last awful fifteen minutes.'

Bride felt that it was time to look about and see if there was no chance of saving himself. He knew that by this time all the boats had gone. He could see, by looking over the side, that the water was far nearer than it had yet been, and that the fo'c'sle decks, which of course were much lower than the superstructure on which the Marconi cabin was situated, were already awash. He remembered that there was a lifebelt for every member of the crew and that his own was under his bunk; and he went and put it on. And then, thinking how cold the water would be, he went back and put his boots on, and an extra coat. Phillips was still standing at the key, talking to the *Olympic* now and telling her the tragic and shameful news that her twin sister, the unsinkable, was sinking by the head and was pretty near her end. While Phillips was sending this message Bride strapped a lifebelt about him and put on his overcoat. Then, at Phillip's suggestion, Bride went out to see if there was anything left in the shape of a boat by which they could get away. He saw some men struggling helplessly with a collapsible boat which they were trying to lower down on to the deck. Bride gave them a hand and then, although it was the last boat left, he resolutely turned his back on it and went back to Phillips. At that moment for the last time, the Captain looked in to give them their release.

'Men, you have done your full duty, you can do no more. Abandon your cabin now; it is every man for himself; you look out for yourselves. I release you. That's the way of it at this kind of time; every man for himself.'

Then happened one of the strangest incidents of that strange hour. I can only give it in Bride's own words:

'Phillips clung on, sending, sending. He clung on for about ten minutes, or maybe fifteen minutes, after the Captain released him. The water was then coming into our cabin.'

'While he worked something happened I hate to tell about. I was back in my room getting Phillips's money for him, and as I looked out of the door I saw a stoker, or somebody from below decks, leaning over Phillips from behind. Phillips was too busy to notice what the man was doing, but he was slipping the lifebelt off Phillips's back. He was a big man, too.'

'As you can see, I'm very small. I don't know what it was I got hold of, but I remembered in a flash the way Phillips had clung on; how I had to fix that lifebelt in place, because he was too busy to do it.'

'I knew that man from below decks had his own lifebelt, and should have known where to get it. I suddenly felt a passion not to let that man die a decent sailor's death. I wished he might have stretched a rope or walked a plank. I did my duty. I hope I finished him, but I don't know.'

'We left him on the cabin floor of the wireless room, and he wasn't moving.'

Phillips left the cabin, running aft, and Bride never saw him alive again. He himself came out and found the water covering the bridge and coming aft over the boat deck.

12

The Band Plays On

There is one other separate point of view from which we may look at the ship during this fateful hour before all points of view become merged in one common experience. Mr Boxhall, the Fourth Officer, who had been on the bridge at the moment of the impact, had been busy sending up rockets and signals in the effort to attract the attention of a ship whose lights could be seen some ten miles away; a mysterious ship which cannot be traced, but whose lights appear to have been seen by many independent witnesses on the *Titanic*. So sure was he of her position that Mr Boxhall spent almost all his time on the bridge signalling to her with rockets and flashes; but no answer was received. He had, however, also been on a rapid tour of inspection of the ship immediately after she had struck. He went down to the steerage quarters forward and aft, and he was also down in the deep forward compartment where the Post Office men were working with the mails, and he had at that time found nothing wrong, and his information contributed much to the sense of security that was spread amongst the passengers.

Mr Pitman, the Third Officer, was in his bunk at the time of the collision, having been on duty on the bridge from six to eight, when the Captain had also been on the bridge. There had been talk of ice among the officers on Sunday, and they had expected to meet with it just before midnight, at the very time, in fact, when they had met with it. But very little ice had been seen, and the speed of the ship had not been reduced. Mr Pitman says that when he awoke he heard a sound which seemed to him to be the sound of the ship coming to anchor. He was not actually awake then, but he had the sensation of the ship halting, and heard a sound like that of chains whirling round the windlass and running through the hawseholes into the water. He lay in bed for three or four minutes wondering in a sleepy sort of way where they could have anchored. Then, becoming more awake, he got up, and without dressing went out on deck; he saw nothing remarkable, but he went back and dressed, suspecting that something was the matter. While he was dressing Mr Boxhall looked in and said: 'We have struck an iceberg, old man; hurry up!'

He also went down below to make an inspection and find out what damage had been done. He went to the forward well deck, where ice was lying, and into the fo'c'sle, but found nothing wrong there. The actual damage was farther aft, and at that time the water had not come into the bows of the ship. As he was going back he met a number of firemen corning up the gangway with their bags of clothing; they told him that water was coming into their place. They were firemen off duty, who afterwards were up on the boat deck helping to man the boats. Then Mr Pitman went down lower into the ship and looked into No. 1 hatch, where he could plainly see water. All this took time; and when he came back he found that the men were beginning to get the boats ready, a task at which he helped under Mr Murdoch's orders. Presently Mr Murdoch ordered him to take command of a boat and hang about aft of the gangway. Pitman had very little relish for leaving the ship at that time, and in spite of the fact that she was taking in water, everyone was convinced that the *Titanic* was a much safer place than the open sea. He had about forty passengers and six of the crew in his boat, and as it was about to be lowered, Mr Murdoch leant over to him and shook him heartily by the hand: 'Goodbye, old man, and good luck,' he said, in tones which rather surprised Pitman, for they seemed to imply that the goodbye might be for a long time. His boat was lowered down into the water, unhooked, and shoved off, and joined the gradually increasing fleet of other boats that were cruising about in the starlight.

There was one man walking about that upper deck whose point of view was quite different from that of anyone else. Mr Bruce Ismay, like so many others, was awakened from sleep by the stopping of the engines; like so many others, also, he lay still for a few moments, and then got up and went into the passageway, where he met a steward and asked him what was the matter. The steward knew nothing, and Mr Ismay went back to his stateroom, put on a dressing gown and slippers, and went up to the bridge, where he saw the Captain. 'What has happened?' he asked. 'We have struck ice,' was the answer. 'Is the injury serious?' 'I think so,' said the Captain. Then Mr Ismay came down in search of the Chief Engineer, whom he met coming up to the bridge; he asked him the same question, and he also said he thought the injury serious. He understood from them that the ship was certainly in danger, but that there was hope that if the pumps could be kept going there would be no difficulty in keeping her afloat quite long enough for help to come and for the passengers to be taken off. Whatever was to be the result, it was a terrible moment for Mr Ismay, a terrible blow to the pride and record of the Company, that this, their greatest and most invulnerable ship, should be at least disabled, and possibly lost, on her maiden voyage. But like a sensible man, he did not stand wringing his hands at the inevitable; he did what he could to reassure the passengers, repeating, perhaps with a slight quaver of doubt in his voice, the old word — unsinkable. When the boats began to be launched he went and tried to help, apparently in his anxiety getting rather in the way. In this endeavour he encountered the wrath of Mr Lowe, the Fifth Officer, who was superintending the launching of boat No. 5. Mr Lowe did not know the identity of the nervous, excited figure standing by the davits, nor recognize the voice which kept saying nervously, 'Lower away! Lower away!' and it was therefore with no misgivings that he ordered him away from the boat, saying brusquely, 'If you will kindly get to hell out of this perhaps I'll be able to do something!' — a trifling incident, but evidence that Mr Ismay made no use of his position for his own personal ends. He said nothing, and went away to another boat, where he succeeded in being more useful, and it was not till afterwards that an awe-stricken steward told the Fifth Officer who it was that he had chased away with such language. But after that Mr Ismay was among the foremost in helping to sort out the women and children and get them expeditiously packed into the boats, with a burden of misery and responsibility on his heart that we cannot measure.

One can imagine a great bustle and excitement while the boats were being sent away; but when they had all gone, and there was nothing more to be done, those who were left began to look about them and realize their position. There was no doubt about it, the *Titanic* was sinking, not with any plunging or violent movement, but steadily settling down, as a rock seems to settle into the water when the tide rises about it.

Down in the engine room and stokeholds in conditions which can hardly be imagined by the ordinary landsman, men were still working with a grim and stoic heroism. The forward stokeholds had been flooded probably an hour after the collision; but it is practically certain that the bulkheads forward of No. 5 held until the last. The doors in those aft of No. 4 had been opened by hand after they had been closed from the bridge, in order to facilitate the passage of the engineering staff about their business; and they remained open, and the principal bulkhead protecting the main engine-room, held until the last. Water thus found its way into some compartments, and gradually rose; but long after those in charge had given up all hope of saving the ship, the stokehold watch were kept hard at work drawing the fires from under the boilers, so that when the water reached them there should be no steam. The duty of the engine room staff was to keep the pumps going as long as possible and to run the dynamos that supplied the current for the light and the Marconi installation. This they did, as the black water rose stage by stage upon them. At least twenty minutes before the ship sank the machinery must have been flooded, and the current for the lights and the wireless supplied from the storage plant. No member of the engine room staff was ever seen alive again, but, when the water finally flooded the stokeholds, the watch were released and told to get up and save themselves if they could.

And up on deck a chilly conviction of doom was slowly but certainly taking the place of that bland confidence in the un-sinkable ship in which the previous hour had been lightly passed. That confidence had been dreadfully overdone, so much so that the stewards had found the greatest difficulty in persuading the passengers to dress themselves and come up on deck, and some who had done so returned to their state rooms and locked themselves in. The last twenty minutes, however, must have shown everyone on deck that there was not a chance left. On a ship as vast and solid as the *Titanic* there is no sensation of actual sinking or settling. She still seemed as immovable as ever, but the water was climbing higher and higher up her black sides. The sensation was not that of the ship sinking, but of the water rising about her, while still visible, still a firm refuge amid the waters, is of the band still playing and a throng of people looking out from the lamp-lit upper decks after the disappearing boats, bracing themselves as best they might for the terrible plunge and shock which they knew was coming. Here and there men who were determined still to make a fight for life climbed over the rail and jumped over; it was not a seventy foot drop now — perhaps under twenty, but it was a formidable jump. Some were stunned and some were drowned at once before the eyes of those who waited; and the dull splashes they made were probably the first visible demonstration of the death that was coming. Duties were still being performed; an old deck steward, who had charge of the chairs, was busily continuing to work, adapting his duties to the emergency that had arisen and lashing chairs together. In this he was helped by Mr Andrews, who was last seen engaged on this strangely ironic task of throwing chairs overboard — frail rafts thrown upon the waters that might or might not avail some struggling soul when the moment should arrive, and the great ship of his designing float no longer. Throughout he had been untiring in his efforts to help and hearten people; but in this the last vision of him, there is something not far short of the sublime.

The last collapsible boat was being struggled with on the upper deck, but there were no seamen about who understood its stiff mechanism; unaccustomed hands fumbled desperately with it, and finally pushed it over the side in its collapsed condition for use as a raft. Many of the seamen and stewards had gathered in the bar room, where the attendant was serving out glasses of whiskey to any and all who came for it; but most men had an instinct against being under cover, and preferred to stand out in the open.

And now those in the boats that had drawn off from the ship could see that the end was at hand. Her bows had gone under, although the stern was still fairly high out of the water. She had sunk down at the forward end of the great superstructure amidships; her decks were just awash, and the black throng was moving aft. The ship was blazing with light, and the strains of the band were faintly heard still playing as they had been commanded to do. But they had ceased to play the jolly rag-time tunes with which the bustle and labour of getting off the boats had been accompanied; solemn strains, the strains of a hymn, could be heard coming over the waters. Many women in the boats, looking back towards that lighted and subsiding mass, knew that somewhere, invisible among the throng, was all that they held dearest in the world waiting for death; and they could do nothing. Some tried to get the crews to turn back, wringing their hands, beseeching, imploring; but no crew dared face the neighbourhood of the giant in her death agony. They could only wait, and shiver, and look.

HEROIC MUSICIANS OF THE TITANIC
who died at their posts like men ~ April 15th 1912

G. KRINS Violin.

W. HARTLEY BANDMASTER.

R. BRICOUX 'Cello

W. T. BRAILEY Piano

P. C. TAYLOR Piano

J. W. WOODWARD Cello

Nearer, my God, to Thee.

Or if on joyful wing cleaving the sky,
Sun, moon and stars forgot, upwards I fly,
Still all my song shall be,
Nearer, my GOD, to Thee, nearer to Thee.

J. F. C. CLARKE

J. L. HUME

40. The band played almost till the end. Led by Wallace Hartley, from Lancashire, whose body was recovered (though not his violin), the band all perished. Their heroism is one of the enduring stories of the sinking of the *Titanic*.

AUTUMN 8.7.8.7. D.

Louis von Esch, c. 1810.

God of mercy and compassion, Look with pity on my pain;

Hear a mournful, broken spirit Prostrate at Thy feet complain;

Many are my foes and mighty; Strength to conquer I have none;

Nothing can uphold my goings But Thy blessed Self alone. AMEN

Saviour, look on Thy beloved,
  Triumph over all my foes;
Turn to heavenly joy my mourning,
  Turn to gladness all my woes;
Live or die, or work or suffer,
  Let my weary soul abide,
In all changes whatsoever,
  Sure and steadfast by Thy side.

When temptations fierce assault me,
  When my enemies I find,
Sin and guilt, and death and Satan,
  All against my soul combined,
Hold me up in mighty waters,
  Keep my eyes on things above—
Rightousness, divine atonement,
  Peace and everlasting love.

41. Logan Marshall's offering for the hymn played as the ship went down, not *Nearer My God to Thee* but the tune *Autumn* as possibly suggested by Harold Bride.

13

'She is Gone': 2.20am Monday 15 April

The end, when it came, was as gradual as everything else had been since the first impact. Just as there was no one moment at which everyone in the ship realized that she had suffered damage; just as there was no one moment when the whole of her company realized that they must leave her; just as there was no one moment when all in the ship understood that their lives were in peril, and no moment when they all knew she must sink; so there was no one moment at which all those left on board could have said, 'She is gone.' At one moment the floor of the bridge, where the Captain stood, was awash; the next a wave came along and covered it with four feet of water, in which the Captain was for a moment washed away, although he struggled back and stood there again, up to his knees in water. 'Boys, you can, do no more,' he shouted, 'look out for yourselves!' Standing near him was a fireman and — strange juxtaposition — two unclaimed solitary little children, scarce more than babies. The fireman seized one in his arms, the Captain another; another wave came and they were afloat in deep water, striking out over the rail of the bridge away from the ship.

The slope of the deck increased, and the sea came washing up against it as waves wash against a steep shore. And then that helpless mass of humanity was stricken at last with the fear of death, and began to scramble madly aft, away from the chasm of water that kept creeping up and up the decks. Then a strange thing happened. They who had been waiting to sink into the sea found themselves rising into the air as the slope of the decks grew steeper. Up and up, dizzily high out of reach of the dark waters into which they had dreaded to be plunged; higher and higher into the air, towards the stars, the stern of the ship rose slowly right out of the water, and hung there for a time that is estimated variously between two and five minutes; a terrible eternity to those who were still clinging. Many, thinking the end had come, jumped; the water resounded with splash after splash as the bodies, like mice shaken out of a trap into a bucket, dropped into the water. All who could do so laid hold of something; ropes, stanchions, deck-houses, mahogany doors, window frames, anything, and so clung on while the stern of the giant ship reared itself towards the sky. Many had no hold, or lost the hold they had, and these slid down the steep smooth decks, as people slide down a water chute into the sea.

We dare not linger here, even in imagination; dare not speculate; dare not look closely, even with the mind's eye, at this poor human agony, this last pitiful scramble for dear life that the serene stars shone down upon. We must either turn our faces away, or withdraw to that surrounding circle where the boats were hovering with their terror-stricken burdens, and see what they saw. They saw the after part of the ship, blazing with light, stand up, a suspended prodigy, between the stars and the waters; they saw the black atoms, each one of which they knew to be a living man or woman on fire with agony, sliding down like shot rubbish into the sea; they saw the giant decks bend and crack; they heard a hollow and tremendous rumbling as the great engines tore themselves

42. Slowly but surely, *Titanic* settled bow first into the water, being dragged inexorably down into the deep. Her lights blazed till almost the end, it was a surreal sight for those in the lifeboats.

43. An artists impression from *L'Illustration* magazine of the escape
from the sinking *Titanic*. The boats start to move away to avoid the
expected suction. However the iceberg in this picture was not seen
when the ship was sinking..

44. A dramatic drawing by the contemporary artist Henry Reuterdahl showing the great ship sinking. Close by, passengers like Bruce Ismay watched on in a state of shock.

45. View from the lifeboats of the *Titanic*.

SETTLES TO FORWARD STACK
BREAKS BETWEEN STACKS

~1:40 A.M.

46. 1.40am *Titanic* settles to forward stack, breaks between stacks.

Funnel for auxiliary Machinery ventilation

SPACE OCCUPIED BY RECIPROCATING & TURBINE ENGINES

WATER LINE

off a Forward Funnels carrying off products of combustion from Main Boilers

SPACE OCCUPIED BY BOILERS

47. To the amazement of the awed watchers in the lifeboats, the doomed vessel remained in an uprighr position for a time estimated at five minutes.

48. Lifeboats pull away from the sinking ship. *Titanic* starts to point skyward before her dive into the abyss.

FORWARD END FLOATS, 'THEN SINKS

1.50 A.M

49. 1.50am *Titanic's* forward end floats then sinks. Jack Thayer (first class passenger, Boat B) was one of a number of survivors to describe the ship breaking in two as she sank. Sketch 4 of 6 of the series of illustrations drawn aboard *Carpathia* clearly show the two halves. It would be over seventy years before Thayer was proved right when the wreck was discovered resting on the seabed in two halves.

STERN SECTION. PIVETS AMIDSHIPS AND SWINGS OVER SPOT WHERE FORWARD SECTION SANK

2.00 A.M

50. 2.00am Stern section of *Titanic* pivots and swings over spot where forward section sank.

LAST POSITION IN WHICH 'TITANIC' STAYED 5 MINUTES BEFORE THE FINAL PLUNGE

L.P. Skidmore
S.S. "Carpathia". Apr 15th 1912.

51. *c.*2.15am Final position in which *Titanic* stayed for 5 minutes before the final plunge.

from their steel beds and crashed through the ship; they saw sparks streaming in a golden rain from one of the funnels; heard the dull boom of an explosion while the spouting funnel fell over into the sea with a slap that killed everyone beneath it and set the nearest boat rocking; heard two more dull bursting reports as the steel bulkheads gave way or decks blew up; saw the lights flicker out, flicker back again, and then go out for ever, and the ship, like some giant sea creature forsaking the strife of the upper elements for the peace of the submarine depths, launched herself with one slow plunge and dive beneath the waves.

There was no great maelstrom as they had feared, but the sea was swelling and sinking all about them; and they could see waves and eddies where rose the imprisoned air, the smoke and steam of vomited-up ashes, and a bobbing commotion of small dark things where the *Titanic*, in her pride and her shame, with the clocks ticking and the fires burning in her luxurious rooms, had plunged down to the icy depths of death.

14

Cries from the Sea

As the ship sank and the commotion and swirl of the waves subsided, the most terrible experience of all began. The seas were not voiceless; the horrified people in the surrounding boats heard an awful sound from the dark central area, a collective voice, compound of moans, shrieks, cries and despairing calls, from those who were struggling in the water. It was an area of death and of agony towards which those in the boats dared not venture, even, although they knew their own friends were perishing and crying for help there. They could only wait and listen, hoping that it might soon be over. But it was not soon over. There was a great deal of floating wreckage to which hundreds of people clung, some for a short time, some for a long time; and while they clung on they cried out to their friends to save them. One boat — that commanded by Mr Lowe, the Fifth Officer — did, after transhipping some of its passengers into other boats, and embarking a crew of oarsmen, venture back into the dark centre of things. The wreckage and dead bodies showed the sea so thickly that they could hardly row without touching a dead body; and once, when they were trying to reach a survivor who was clinging to a piece of broken staircase, praying and calling for help, it took them nearly half an hour to cover the fifty feet that separated them from him, so thick were the bodies. This reads like an exaggeration, but it is well attested. The water was icy cold, and benumbed many of them, who thus died quickly; a few held on to life, moaning, wailing, calling — but in vain.

A few strong men were still making a desperate fight for life. The collapsible boat, which Bride had seen a group of passengers attempting to launch a few minutes before the ship sank, was washed off by a wave in its collapsed condition. Such boats contain air compartments in their bottom, and thus, even although they are not opened, they float like rafts, and can carry a considerable weight. Some of those who were swept off the ship by the same wave that took the boat found themselves near it and climbed on to it. Mr Lightoller, the Second Officer, had dived as the ship dived, and been sucked down the steep submerged wall of the hull against the grating over the blower for the exhaust steam. Far down under the water he felt the force of an explosion which blew him up to the surface, where he breathed for a moment, and was then sucked back by the water washing into the ship as it sank. This time he landed against the grating over the pipes that furnished the draught for the funnels, and stuck there. There was another explosion, and again he came to the surface not many feet from the ship, and found himself near the collapsible boat, to which he clung. It was quite near him that the huge funnel fell over into the water and killed many swimmers before his eyes. He drifted for a time on the collapsible boat, until he was taken off into one of the lifeboats.

Bride also found himself strangely involved with this boat, which he had last seen on the deck of the ship. When he was swept off, he found himself in the horrible position of being trapped under water beneath this boat. He struggled out and tried to climb on to it, but it took him a long time; at last, however, he managed to get up on it, and found five or six other people there. And now and then some other swimmer stronger than most, would come up and be helped on board. Some thus helped died almost immediately; there were four found dead upon this boat when at last the survivors were rescued.

There was another boat also not far off, a lifeboat, capsized likewise. Six men managed to scramble on to the keel of this craft; it was almost all she could carry. Mr Caldwell, a second class passenger, who had been swimming about in the icy water for nearly an hour, with dead bodies floating all about him, was beginning to despair when he found himself near a crate to which another man was clinging. 'Will it hold two?' he asked. And the other man, with a rare heroism, said: 'Catch hold and try; we will live or die together.' And these two, clinging precariously to the crate, reached the overturned lifeboat and were hauled up to its keel. Presently another man came swimming along and asked if they could take him on but the boat was already dangerously loaded; the weight of another man would have meant death for all, and they told him so. 'All right,' he cried, 'goodbye; God bless you all!' And he sank before their eyes.

Captain Smith, who had last been seen washed from the bridge as the ship sank, with a child in his arms, was seen once more before he died. He was swimming, apparently only in the hope of saving the child that he held; for in his austere conception of his duty there was no place of salvation for him while others were drowning and struggling. He swam up to a boat with the child and gasped out: 'Take the child!' A dozen willing hands were stretched out to take it, and then to help him into the boat; but he shook them off.

Only for a moment he held on, asking: 'What became of Murdoch?' and when they said that he was dead, he let go his hold, saying: 'Let me go'; and the last that they saw of him was swimming back towards the ship. He had no lifebelt; he had evidently no wish that there should be any gruesome resurrection of his body from the sea, and undoubtedly he found his grave where he wished to find it, somewhere hard by the grave of his ship.

The irony of chance, the merciless and illogical selection which death makes in a great collective disaster, was exemplified over and over again in the deaths of people who had escaped safely to a boat, and the salvation of others who were involved in the very centre of destruction. The strangest escape of all was probably that of Colonel Gracie of the United States army, who jumped from the topmost deck of the ship when she sank and was sucked down with her. He was drawn down for a long while, and whirled round and round, and would have been drawn down to a depth from which he could never have come up alive if it had not been for the explosion which took place after the ship sank. 'After sinking with the ship.' he says, 'it appeared to me as if I was propelled by some great force through the water. This may have been caused by explosions under the waters, and I remembered fearful stories of people being boiled to death. Innumerable thoughts of a personal nature, having relation to mental telepathy, flashed through my brain. I thought of those at home, as if my spirit might go to them to say goodbye. Again and again I prayed for deliverance, although I felt sure that the end had come. I had the greatest difficulty in holding my breath until I came to the surface. I knew that once I inhaled, the water would suffocate me. I struck out with all my strength for the surface. I got to the air again after

52. Colonel Gracie was in the water for a short while, being sucked down with the ship but luckily escaping the suction as she sank. He found himself some distance from an upturned collapsible boat, and, with a few, others, successfully managed to remain on the collapsible until taken into lifeboat 12 later that morning.

53. One of *Titanic*'s lifeboats.

54. One of *Titanic*'s lifeboats approaches the *Carpathia*.

55. Lifeboat 14 towing collapsable D.

Above: 56. *Titanic* survivors in collapsable lifeboat D.

Left: 57. The Countess of Rothes (first class passenger, lifeboat 8) was from Prinknash Abbey, in Gloucestershire, where a memorial exists to the *Titanic*.

a time that seemed to me unending. There was nothing in sight save the ocean strewn with great masses of wreckage, dying men and women all about me, groaning and crying piteously. I saw wreckage everywhere, and what came within reach I clung to. I moved from one piece to another until I reached the collapsible boat. She soon became so full that it seemed as if she would sink if more came on board her. We had to refuse to let any others climb on board. This was the most pathetic and horrible scene of all. The piteous cries of those around us ring in my ears, and I will remember them to my dying day. "Hold on to what you have, old boy," we shouted to each man who tried to get on board. "One more of you would sink us all." Many of those whom we refused answered, as they went to their death, "Good luck; God bless you." All the time we were buoyed up and sustained by the hope of rescue. We saw lights in all directions — particularly some green lights which, as we learned later, were rockets burned by one of the *Titanic's* boats. So we passed the night with the waves washing over and burying our raft deep in the water.'

It was twenty minutes past two when the *Titanic* sank, two hours and forty minutes after she had struck the iceberg; and for two hours after that the boats drifted all round and about, some of them in bunches of three or four, others solitary. Almost every kind of suffering was endured in them, although, after the mental horrors of the preceding hour, physical sufferings were scarcely felt. Some of the boats bad hardly anyone but women in them; in many the stokers and stewards were quite useless at the oars. But here and there, in that sorrowful, horror-stricken company, heroism lifted its head and human nature took heart again. Women took their turn at the oars in boats where the men were either too few or incapable of rowing; and one woman notably, the Countess of Rothes, practically took command of her boat and was at an oar all the time. Where they were rowing to most of them did not know. They had seen lights at the time the ship went down, and some of them made for these; but they soon disappeared, and probably most of the boats were following each other aimlessly, led by one boat in which some green flares were found, which acted as a beacon for which the others made. One man had a pocket electric lamp, which he flashed now and then, a little ray of hope and guidance shining across those dark and miserable waters. Not all of the boats had food and water on board. Many women were only in their nightclothes, some of the men in evening dress; everyone was bitterly cold, although, fortunately, there was no wind and no sea.

The stars paled in the sky; the darkness became a little lighter the gray daylight began to come. Out of the surrounding gloom a wider and wider area of sea became visible, with here and there a boat discernible on it, and here and there some fragments of wreckage. By this time the boats had rowed away from the dreadful region, and but few floating bodies were visible. The waves rose and fell, smooth as oil, first gray in colour, and then, as the light increased, the pure dark blue of mid-ocean. The eastern sky began to grow red under the cloud bank, and from red to orange, and from orange to gold, the lovely pageantry of an Atlantic dawn began to unfold itself before the aching eyes that had been gazing on prodigies and horrors. From out that well of light in the sky came rays that painted the wave-backs first with rose, and then with saffron, and then with pure gold. And in the first flush of that blessed and comforting light the draggled and weary sufferers saw, first a speck far to the south, then a smudge of cloud, and then the red and black smokestack of a steamer that meant succour and safety for them.

15

Saviour of the Survivors:
Captain Rostron of the *Carpathia*

From every quarter of the ocean, summoned by the miracle of the wireless voice, many ships had been racing since midnight to the help of the doomed liner. From midnight onwards captains were being called by messages from the wireless operators of their ships, telling them that the *Titanic* was asking for help; courses were being altered and chief engineers called upon to urge their stoke-hold crews to special efforts; for coal means steam, and steam means speed, and speed may mean life. Many ships that could receive the strong electric impulses sent out from the *Titanic* had not electric strength enough to answer; but they turned and came to that invisible spot represented by a few figures which the faithful wireless indicated. Even as far as five hundred miles away, the *Parisian* turned in her tracks in obedience to the call and came racing towards the north-west. But there were tragedies even with the wireless. The Leyland liner *Californian*, bound for Boston, was only seventeen miles away from the *Titanic* when she struck, and could have saved every soul on board; but her wireless apparatus was not working, and she was deaf to the agonized calls that were being sent out from only a few miles away. The *Parisian*, five hundred miles away, could hear and come, though it was useless; the

Californian could not hear and so did not come though, if she had, she would probably have saved every life on board. The *Cincinnati*, the *Amerika*, the *Prinz Friedrich Wilhelm*, the *Menominee*, the *La Provence*, the *Prinz Adalbert*, the *Virginian*, the *Olympic*, and the *Baltic* all heard the news and all turned towards Lat. 41° 46' N., Long. 50° 14' W. The dread news was being whispered all over the sea, and even ashore, just as the dwellers on the North Atlantic seaboard were retiring to rest, the station at Cape Race intercepted the talk of the *Titanic* 270 miles away, and flashed the message out far and wide; so that Government tugs and ships with steam up in harbours, and everything afloat in the vicinity which heard the news might hurry to the rescue. Cape Race soon heard that the *Virginian* was on her way to the *Titanic's* position, then that the *Olympic* and *Carpathia* had altered their courses and were making for the wounded ship, and so on. Throughout the night the rumours in the air were busy, while still the steady calls came out in firm electric waves from the *Titanic* still calling, still flashing 'C. Q. D.' At 1.20 she whispered to the *Olympic*, 'Get your boats ready; going down fast by the head.' At 1.35 the *Frankfurt* (after an hour and a half's delay) said, 'We are starting for you.' Then at 1.41 came a message to the *Olympic*, 'C.Q.D., boilers flooded.'

'Are there any boats round you already?' asked the *Olympic*; but there was no answer.

Other ships began to call, giving encouraging messages: 'We are coming,' said the *Birma*, 'only fifty miles away'; but still there was no answer.

All over the North Atlantic men in lighted instrument rooms sat listening with the telephones at their ears; they heard each other's questions and waited in the silence, but it was never broken again by the voice from the *Titanic*.

'All quiet now,' reported the *Birma* to the *Olympic*; and all quiet it was, except for the thrashing and pounding of a score of propellers, and the hiss of a dozen steel stems as they ripped the smooth waters on courses converging to the spot where the wireless voice had suddenly flickered out into silence.

But of all those who had been listening to the signals Captain Rostron of the *Carpathia* knew that his ship would most likely be among the first to reach the spot. It was about midnight on Sunday that the passengers of the *Carpathia* first became aware that something unusual was happening. The course had been changed and a certain hurrying about on the decks took the place of the usual midnight quiet. The trembling and vibration increased to a quick jumping movement as pressure of steam was gradually increased and the engines urged to the extreme of their driving capacity. The chief steward summoned his staff and set them to work making sandwiches and preparing hot drinks. All the hot water was cut off from the cabins and bathrooms, so that every ounce of steam could be utilized for driving the machinery.

The *Carpathia* was nearly seventy miles from the position of the *Titanic* when she changed her course and turned northward; she had been steaming just over four hours when, in the light of that wonderful dawn, those on the lookout descried a small boat. As they drew nearer they saw other boats, and fragments of wreckage, and masses of ice drifting about the sea. Captain Rostron stopped while he was still a good distance from, the boats, realizing that preparations must be made before he could take passengers on board. The accommodation gangway was rigged and also rope ladders lowered over the sides, and canvas slings were arranged to hoist up those who were too feeble to climb. The passengers crowded along the rail or looked out of their portholes to see the reaping of this strange harvest of the sea. The first boat came up almost filled with women and children — women in evening dress or in fur coats thrown over nightgowns, in silk stockings and slippers, in rags and shawls. The babies were crying; some of the women were injured and some half-fainting; all had horror on their faces. Other boats began to come up, and the work of embarking the seven hundred survivors went on. It took a long time, for some of the boats were far away, and it was not until they had been seven hours afloat that the last of them were taken on board the *Carpathia*. Some climbed up the ladders, others were put into the slings and swung on board, stewards standing by with rum and brandy to revive the fainting; and many willing hands were occupied with caring for the sufferers, taking them at once to improvised couches and beds, or conducting those who were not so exhausted to the saloon where hot drinks and food were ready. But it was a ghastly company. As boat after boat came up, those who had already been saved eagerly searched among its occupants to see if their own friends were among them; and as gradually the tale of boats was completed and it was known that no more had been saved, and the terrible magnitude of the loss was realized then, in the words of one of the *Carpathia's* people, 'Bedlam broke loose.' Women who had borne themselves bravely throughout the hours of waiting and exposure broke into shrieking hysterics, calling upon the names of their lost. Some went clean out of their minds; one or two died there in the very moment of rescue. The *Carpathia's* passengers gave up their rooms and ransacked their trunks to find clothing for the more than half-naked survivors; and at last exhaustion, resignation, and the doctor's merciful drugs did the rest. The dead were buried; those who had been snatched too late from the bitter waters were committed to them again, and eternally, with solemn words; and the *Carpathia* was headed for New York.

58 & 59. *Titanic* passengers coming aboard the *Carpathia*.

60. The survivors reached the *Carpathia* early next morning and were hauled aboard the gallant Cunarder. The youngest, Millvina Dean was pulled up in a sack.

Opposite page: 61. *Titanic* lifeboat alongside the *Carpathia*. The gangway doors are open to facilitate access.

62, 63 & 64. Groups of *Titanic* survivors aboard rescue ship *Carpathia*.

65. Groups of *Titanic* survivors aboard rescue ship *Carpathia*: George Harder and his wife Dorothy Harder (first class passengers, both rescued on lifeboat 5). The Harders were a honeymoon couple saved from the *Titanic*. The woman weeping, with hand to her face, is Clara Hays (first class passenger, lifeboat 3) her husband Charles M. Hays perished. When the cry came to get in the lifeboats the Harders, thinking there was no danger, jumped in the first boat lowered.

66. Captain Arthur Henry Rostron who rushed his ship *Carpathia* to the rescue of *Titanic's* survivors and brought them to New York.

67. The Cunard Line steamship *Carpathia* which heard the wireless call of distress from the *Titanic* and was the first to reach the scene of the disaster and take on board survivors.

68. Arrival of the *Carpathia* into New York on Thursday 18 April 1912. *Carpathia* dropped off the empty *Titanic* lifeboats at Pier 59, as property of the White Star Line, before unloading the survivors at Pier 54 where thousands of friends and relatives of the survivors were waiting.

16

Final Destination, New York: Evening, Thursday 18 April

The *Californian* had come up while the *Carpathia* was taking the survivors on board, and it was arranged that she should remain and search the vicinity while the *Carpathia* made all haste to New York. And the other ships that had answered the call for help either came up later in the morning and stayed for a little cruising about in the forlorn hope of finding more survivors, or else turned back and resumed their voyages when they heard the *Carpathia's* tidings.

In the meantime the shore stations could get no news. Word reached New, York and London in the course of the morning that the *Titanic* had struck an iceberg and was badly damaged, but nothing more was known until a message, the origin of which could not be discovered, came to say that the *Titanic* was being towed to Halifax by the *Virginian,* and that all her passengers were saved. With this news the London evening papers came out on that Monday, and even on Tuesday the early editions of the morning papers had the same story, and commented upon the narrow escape of the huge ship. Even the White Star officials had on Monday no definite news and when their offices in New York were besieged by newspaper men and relatives of the passengers demanding information, the pathetic belief in the *Titanic's* strength was allowed to overshadow anxieties concerning the greater disaster. Mr Franklin, the vice-president of the American Trust to which the White Star Company belongs, issued the following statement from New York on Monday:

We have nothing direct from the *Titanic*, but are perfectly satisfied that the vessel is unsinkable. The fact that the Marconi messages have ceased means nothing; it may be due to atmospheric conditions or the coming up of the ships or something of that sort.

We are not worried over the possible loss of the ship, as she will not go down, but we are sorry for any inconvenience caused to the traveling public. We are absolutely certain that the *Titanic* is able to

69. P.A.S. Franklin, White Star Line Vice President. Yet, when the New York office of the White Star Line was informed that *Titanic* was in trouble, White Star Line Vice President P.A.S. Franklin announced 'We place absolute confidence in the *Titanic*. We believe the boat is unsinkable.' By the time Franklin spoke those words *Titanic* was at the bottom of the ocean.

withstand any damage. She may be down by the head, but would float indefinitely in that condition.

Still the same word, 'unsinkable,' which had now indeed for the first time been a true one: for it is only when she lies at the bottom

70. Newspaper headline, Tuesday 16 April 1912.

of the sea that any ship can be called unsinkable. On Tuesday morning when the dreadful news was first certainly known, those proud words had to be taken back. Again Mr Franklin had to face the reporters, and this time he could only say:

> I must take upon myself the whole blame for that statement. I made it, and I believed it when I made it. The accident to the *Olympic*, when she collided with the cruiser *Hawke*, convinced me that these ships, the *Olympic* and *Titanic*, were built like battleships, able to resist almost any kind of accident, particularly a collision. I made the statement in good faith, and upon me must rest the responsibility for error, since the fact has proved that it was not a correct description of the unfortunate *Titanic*.

And for three days while the *Carpathia* was ploughing her way, now slowly through ice-strewn seas, and now at full speed through open water, and while England lay under the cloud of an unprecedented disaster, New York was in ferment of grief, excitement, and indignation. Crowds thronged the streets outside the offices of the White Star Line, while gradually, in lists of thirty or forty at a time, the names of the survivors began to come through from the *Carpathia*. And at last, when all the names had been spelled out, and interrogated, and corrected, the grim total of the figures stood out in appalling significance — seven hundred and three saved, one thousand five hundred and three lost.

It is not possible, nor would it be very profitable, to describe the scenes that took place on these days of waiting, the alternations of hope and grief, of thankfulness and wild despair, of which the shipping offices were the scene. They culminated on the Thursday evening when the *Carpathia* arrived in New York. The greatest precautions had been taken to prevent the insatiable thirst for news from turning that solemn disembarkation into a battlefield. The entrance to the dock was carefully guarded, and only those were admitted who had business there or who could prove that they had relations among the rescued passengers. Similar precautions were taken on the ship; she was not even boarded by the Custom officials, nor were any reporters allowed on board, although a fleet of steam launches went out in the cold rainy evening to meet her, bearing pressmen who were prepared to run any risks to get a footing on the ship. They failed, however, and the small craft were left behind in the mist, as the *Carpathia* came gliding up the Hudson.

Among the waiting crowd were nurses, doctors, and a staff of ambulance men and women; for all kinds of wild rumours were afloat as to the condition of those who had been rescued. The women of New York had devoted the days of waiting to the organization of a powerful relief committee, and had collected money and clothing on an ample scale to meet the needs of those, chiefly among the steerage passengers, who should find themselves destitute when they

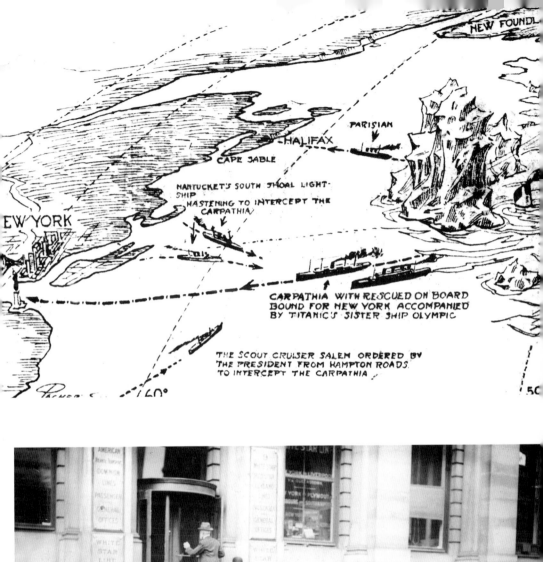

PARISIAN

NEW FOUNDL

HALIFAX

CAPE SABLE

NANTUCKET'S SOUTH SHOAL LIGHT-
SHIP
HASTENING TO INTERCEPT THE
CARPATHIA

EW YORK

CARPATHIA WITH RESCUED ON BOARD
BOUND FOR NEW YORK ACCOMPANIED
BY TITANIC'S SISTER SHIP OLYMPIC

THE SCOUT CRUISER SALEM ORDERED BY
THE PRESIDENT FROM HAMPTON ROADS.
TO INTERCEPT THE CARPATHIA

60°

VIRGINIA RESUMES VOYAGE
TO LIVERPOOL

Opposite page top: 71. A contemporary newspaper depiction of the location of the sinking of the *Titanic* and positions of other ships in the area.

Opposite page bottom: 72. Getting *Titanic* news. White Star Office, April 1912.

Right: 73. A photograph of Mrs Benjamin Guggenheim leaving the White Star offices in New York after trying to get news of her husband. He had dressed in his best before going down with the ship.

74. Seeking information about lost relatives and friends at the office of the steamship company in New York.

75. Interior of the Cunard Line pier all cleared out ready to receive the survivors of the *Titanic* on arrival of the *Carpathia*, where they were met by relatives, doctors and nurses.

76. Crowd awaiting survivors from the *Titanic* 18 April 1912.

77. The *Titanic's* 13 surviving lifeboats in New York. Their nameplates and White Star flags were removed and the lifeboats disappeared.

landed. And there, in the rain of that gloomy evening, they waited.

At last they saw the *Carpathia* come creeping up the river and head towards the White Star pier. The flashlights of photographers were playing about her, and with this silent salute she came into dock. Gateways had been erected, shutting off the edge of the pier from the sheds in which the crowd was waiting, and the first sight they had of the rescued was when after the gangway had been rigged, and the brief formalities of the shore complied with, the passengers began slowly to come down the gangway. A famous English dramatist who was looking on at the scene has written of it eloquently, describing the strange varieties of bearing and demeanour; how one face had a startled, frightened look that seemed as if it would always be there, another a set and staring gaze; how one showed an angry, rebellious desperation, and another seemed merely dazed. Some carried on stretchers, some supported by nurses, and some handed down by members of the crew, they came, either to meetings that were agonizing in their joy, or to blank loneliness that would last until they died. Five or six babies without mothers, some of them utterly unidentified and unidentifiable, were handed down with the rest, so strangely preserved, in all their tenderness and helplessness, through that terrible time of confusion and exposure.

And in the minds of those who looked on at this sad procession there was one tragic, recurrent thought: that for everyone who came down the gangway, ill perhaps, maimed perhaps, destitute perhaps, but alive and on solid earth again, there were two either drifting in the slow Arctic current, or lying in the great submarine valley to which the ship had gone down. They were a poor remnant indeed of all that composite world of pride, and strength, and riches; for Death winnows with a strange fan, and although one would suit his purpose as well as an other, he often chooses the best and the

78. Harold Bride (lifeboat B), surviving wireless operator of the *Titanic*, with feet bandaged, being carried up ramp of ship. He was washed off the deck of the *Titanic* just as it sank but managed to attach himself to the upturned hull of Collapsible B.

79. A happier picture of the second class child passengers French brothers Michel (age 4) and Edmond Navratil (age 2) in the care of fellow *Titanic* survivor, Margaret Hays. Miss Hays escaped on lifeboat 7 but volunteered once on board *Carpathia* to care for the 'orphans' as she could speak fluent French. They escaped the sinking ship in Collapsible D, their father perished.

80. Stuart Collett (second class passenger, lifeboat 9) one of the *Titanic* survivors arriving in New York on the *Carpathia*.

81. Frederick Fleet (lifeboat 6), Lookout on the *Titanic* who spotted the iceberg.

New-York Tribune.

ᴠᴏʟ. LXXII... N° 23,896. To-day, cloudy. To-morrow, fair; east winds. NEW-YORK, FRIDAY, APRIL 19, 1912.—SIXTEEN PAGES. • • PRICE ONE CENT In City of New York Jersey City and Hoboken. ᴇʟꜱᴇᴡʜᴇʀᴇ ᴛᴡᴏ ᴄᴇɴᴛꜱ.

HIT BERG AT 21-KNOT SPEED

CARPATHIA'S STORY OF TITANIC'S LOSS, WITH THRILLING DETAILS OF RESCUE

82. Newspaper headline, Friday 19 April 1912.

strongest. There were card-sharpers, and orphaned infants, and destitute consumptives among the saved; and there were hundreds of heroes and strong men among the drowned. There were among the saved those to whom death would have been no great enemy, who had no love for life or ties to bind them to it; and there were those among the drowned for whom life was at its very best and dearest; lovers and workers in the very morning of life before whom the years had stretched forward rich with promise.

And when nearly all had gone and the crowd in the docks was melting away, one man, who had until then remained secluded in the ship came quietly out, haggard and stricken with woe: Bruce Ismay, the representative and figure-head of that pride and power which had given being to the *Titanic*. In a sense he bore on his own shoulders the burden of every sufferer's grief and loss; and he bore it, not with shame, for he had no cause for shame, but with reticence of words and activity in such alleviating deeds as were possible, and with a dignity which was proof against even the bitter injustice of which he was the victim in the days that followed. There, was pity enough in New York, hysterical pity, sentimental pity, real pity, practical pity, for all the obvious and patent distress of the bereaved and destitute; but there was no pity for this man who, of all that ragged remnant that walked back to life down the *Carpathia's* gangway, had perhaps the most need of pity.

17

Heroes

The symbols of Honour and Glory and Time that looked so handsome in the flooding sunlight of the *Titanic's* stairway lie crushed into unrecognizable shapes and splinters beneath the tonnage of two thousand fathoms of ocean water. Time is no more for the fifteen hundred souls who perished with them; but Honour and Glory, by strange ways and unlooked for events, have come into their own. It was not Time, nor the creatures and things of Time that received their final crown there; but things that have nothing to do with Time, qualities that, in their power of rising beyond all human limitations, we must needs call divine.

The *Titanic* was in more senses than one a fool's paradise. There is nothing that man can build that nature cannot destroy, and far as he may advance in might and knowledge and cunning, her blind strength will always be more than his match. But men easily forget this they wish to forget it; and the beautiful and comfortable and agreeable equipment of this ship helped them to forget it. You may cover the walls of a ship with rare woods and upholster them with tapestries and brocades, but it is the bare steel walls behind them on which you depend to keep out the water; it is the strength of those walls, relatively to the strength of such natural forces as may be arrayed against them, on which the safety of the ship depends.

If they are weaker than something which assails them, the water must come in and the ship must sink. It was assumed too readily that, in the case of the *Titanic* these things could not happen; it was assumed too readily that if in the extreme event they did happen, the manifold appliances for saving life would be amply sufficient for the security of the passengers. Thus they lived in a serene confidence such as no ship's company ever enjoyed before, or will enjoy again for a long time to come. And there were gathered about them almost all those accessories of material life which are necessary to the paradise of fools; and are extremely agreeable to wiser men.

It was this: perfect serenity of their condition; which made so poignant the tragedy of their sudden meeting with death — that pale angel whom every man knows that he must some day encounter, but whom most of us hope to find at the end of some road a very long way off waiting for his with comforting and soothing hands. We not expect to meet him suddenly turning the corner of the street, or in an environment of refined and elegant conviviality, or in the midst of our noonday activities, or at midnight on the high seas when we are dreaming on feather pillows. But it was thus that those on the *Titanic* encountered him, waiting there in the ice and the starlight, arresting the ship's progress with his outstretched arm, and standing by, waiting, while the sense of his cold presence gradually sank like a frost into their hearts.

To say that all the men who died on the *Titanic* were heroes would be as absurd as to say that all who were saved were cowards. There were heroes among both groups and cowards among both groups, as there must be among any large number of men. It is the collective behaviour and the general attitude towards disaster that is important at such a time; and in this respect there is ample evidence that death scored no advantage in the encounter, and that, though he too a spoil of bodies that had been destined for him since the moment of their birth, he left the hearts unconquered. So that last half-hour before the end, when everyone on the ship was under sentence of death, modern civilization went through a severe test. By their bearing in that moment those fated men and women had to determine whether, through the long years of peace and increase of material comfort and withdrawal from contact with the cruder elements of life, their race had deteriorated in courage and morale. It is only by such great tests that we can determine how we stand in these matters, and, as they periodically recur, measure our advance or decline. And the human material there made the test a very severe one; for there were people on the *Titanic* who had so entrenched themselves behind ramparts of wealth and influence as to have well nigh forgotten that, equally with the waif and the pauper, they were exposed to the caprice of destiny; and who might have been forgiven if, in that awful moment of realisation, they had shown the white feather and given themselves over to panic. But there is ample evidence that these men stood the test equally as well as those whose occupation and training made them familiar with the risks of the sea, to which they were continually exposed, and through which they might reasonably expect to come to just such an end. There was no theatrical heroism, no striking of attitudes, or attempt to escape from the dread reality in any form of spiritual hypnosis; they simply stood about the decks, smoking cigarettes, talking to one another, and waiting for their hour to strike. There is nothing so hard, nothing so entirely dignified, as to be silent and quiet in the face of an approaching horror.

That was one form of heroism, which will make the influence of this thing deathless long after the memory of it has faded as completely from the minds of men as sight or sign of it has faded from that area of ocean where, two miles above the sunken ship, the rolling blue furrows have smoothed away all trace of the struggles and agonies that embittered it. But there was another heroism which must be regarded as the final crown and glory of this catastrophe — not because it is exceptional, for happily it is not, but because it continued and confirmed a tradition of English sea life that should be a tingling inspiration to everyone who has knowledge of it. The men who did, the work of the ship were no composite, highly drilled body like the men in the navy who, isolated for months at a time and austerely disciplined, are educated into an *esprit de corps* and sense of responsibility that make them willing, in moments of emergency to sacrifice individual safety to the honour of the ship and of the Service to which they belong. These stokers, stewards, and seamen were the ordinary scratch crew, signed on at Southampton for one round trip to New York and back; most of them had never seen each other or their officers before; they had none of the training or the securities afforded by a great national service; they were simply — especially in the case of the stokers — men so low in the community that they were able to live no pleasanter life than that afforded by the stoke hold of a ship an inferno of darkness and noise and commotion and insufferable heat — men whose experience of the good things of life was half an hour's breathing of the open sea air between their spells of labour at the furnaces, or a drunken spree ashore whence, after being poisoned by cheap drink and robbed by joyless women of the fruits of their spell of labour, they are obliged to return to it again to find the means for another debauch. Not the stuff out of which one would expect an austere heroism to be evolved. Yet such are the traditions of the seal such is the power of those traditions

83. A contemporary picture lionising the bravery of the men on the *Titanic*. The myth of male sacrifice developed as the world tried to make sense of the disaster. In practice, some men were much more heroic than others.

84. A drawing from Punch which was dedicated to the 'brave men' who perished in the disaster. Britannia looks on as a grieving woman tries to cope with the immensity of the tragedy. In practice, nearly 50 first class male passengers survived, most controversially Bruce Ismay.

85. The Whited Sepulchre, a contemporary cartoon weighing up the *Titanic's* luxuries against the lives of some of her prominent passengers.

86. *Which? fate or economy in life boats?* by W. A. Rogers (1854-1931) published in *New York Herald*, 17 April 1912.

Above: 87. Photo shows Captain Arthur Rostron and officers of *Carpathia* next to the silver loving cup presented to him in May 1912 by survivors of the *Titanic* in recognition of his heroism in their rescue.

Below: 88. Senate Investigating Committee questioning Harold Cottam at the Waldorf Astoria 29 May 1912. Harold Cottam, wireless operator on the *Carpathia* on the night of the *Titanic* struck an iceberg. It was he who alerted Captain Rostron who turned round the ship and put on all possible speed, and the *Carpathia* was the first ship on the scene of the tragedy.

Right: 89. First class passenger, Madeleine Astor (lifeboat 4). The eighteen year old bride of the millionaire John Astor who went down with the *Titanic* was pregnant at the time of the sinking and went on to give birth to a John Astor's son in August 1912. At one stage whilst waiting on the boat deck, the Astors retired to the gym and sat on the mechanical horses.

and the spirit of those who interpret them, that some of these men — not all, but some — remained down in the *Titanic's* stoke holds long after she had struck, and long after the water, pouring like a cataract through the rent in her bottom and rising like a tide round the black holes where they worked, had warned them that her doom, and probably theirs, was sealed.

In the engine room were another group of heroes, men of a far higher type, with fine intelligences, trained in all the subtleties and craft of modern ships, men with education and imagination who could see in their mind's eye all the variations of horror that might await them. These men also continued at their routine tasks in the engine room, knowing perfectly well that no power on earth could save them, choosing to stay there while there was work to be done for the common good, their best hope being presently to be drowned instead of being boiled or scalded to death. All through the ship, though in less awful circumstances, the same spirit was being observed; men who had duties to do went on doing them because they were the kind of men to whom in such an hour it came more easily to perform than to shirk their duties. The three ship's boys spent the whole of that hour carrying provisions from the store room to the deck; the post office employees worked in the flooded mailroom below to save the mailbags and carry them up to where they might he taken of if there should be a chance; the purser and his men brought up the ship's books and money, against all possibility of its being any use to do so, but because it was their duty at such a time to do so; the stewards were busy to the end with their domestic, and the officers with their executive, duties. In all this we have an example of spontaneous discipline — for they had never been drilled in doing these things, they only knew that they had to do them — such as no barrack-room discipline in the

IN MEMORY
OF THE
HEROIC MUSICIANS
OF THE S.S "TITANIC".
LOST ON HER MAIDEN VOYAGE FROM SOUTHAMPTON TO NEW YORK
APRIL 15th 1912

W. HARTLEY

C. KRINS.   R. BRICOUX

W. T. BRAILEY   J. WOODWARD

90. The Musicians Memorial in Southampton; this photograph is of a replica, the original was destroyed by a Luftwaffe bombing raid in the Second World War.

91. The 'unsinkable' Margaret 'Molly' Brown (first class passenger, lifeboat 6).

92. The *Titanic* memorial a granite statue in Washington DC that honours the men who gave their lives so that women and children might be saved.

world could match such moments all artificial bonds are useless. It is what men are in themselves that determines their conduct and discipline and conduct like this are proofs, not of the superiority of one race over another, but that in the core of human nature itself there is an abiding sweetness and soundness that fear cannot embitter nor death corrupt.

The twin gray horses are still at their work in Belfast Lough, and on any summer morning you may see their white manes shining like gold as they escort you in from the sunrise and the open seat to where the smoke rises and the smoke rises and the din resounds.

For the iron forest has branched again, and its dreadful groves are echoing anew to the clamour of the hammers and the drills, another ship, greater and stronger even than the lost one, is rising within the cathedral scaffolding; and the men who build her, companions of whose whom the *Titanic* spilled into the sea, speak among themselves and say, 'this time we shall prevail.'

List of Illustrations

JR2196b98p201ML 1912.

34. The scenes aboard as women were ushered to the lifeboats. In practice, much of the loading was much less orderly than this. © J & C McCutcheon Collection.

35. The male passengers wish their sweethearts goodbye. Some women chose to remain with their menfolk and take the chance onboard ship. © J & C McCutcheon Collection.

36. It was 75ft from the boat deck to the calm seas below. Many boats left only part full. Of the 1,000 possible lives that could have been saved, only just over 700 actually survived the sinking . © J & C McCutcheon Collection.

37. Heart breaking farewells. Romanticised view of the scene on the Boat Deck as husbands and wives were parted from the 1912 account by Logan Marshall. © Jonathan Reeve JR2175b98fp41 1912.

38. Wireless operator sending messages. But for the wireless, the *Titanic's* passengers would surely have all been lost, as they could not have survived on the Atlantic in the small lifeboats for long. © Jonathan Reeve JR2136f126 1912.

39. A chart from the magazine *The Sphere* showing the ships too far away to help the *Titanic*. Note that the *Californian* is said to be 19½ miles away and there is a mystery ship between her and the stricken liner. © W.B. Bartlett & the Amberley Archive.

40. The band played almost till the end. Led by Wallace Hartley, from Lancashire, whose body was recovered (though not his violin), the band all perished. Their heroism is one of the enduring stories of the sinking of the *Titanic*. © J & C McCutcheon Collection.

41. Logan Marshall's offering for the hymn played as the ship went down, not *Nearer My God to Thee* but the tune *Autumn* as possibly suggested by Harold Bride. © W.B. Bartlett & the Amberley Archive.

42. Slowly but surely, *Titanic* settled bow first into the water, being dragged inexorably down into the deep. Her lights blazed till almost the end, it was a surreal sight for those in the lifeboats. © J & C McCutcheon Collection.

43. An artists impression from *L'Illustration* magazine of the escape from the sinking *Titanic*. The boats start to move away to avoid the expected suction. However the iceberg in this picture was not seen when the ship was sinking.. © J & C McCutcheon Collection. © J & C McCutcheon Collection.

44. A dramatic drawing by the contemporary artist Henry Reuterdahl showing the great ship sinking. Close by, passengers like Bruce Ismay watched on in a state of shock. © W.B. Bartlett & the Amberley Archive.

45. View from the lifeboats of the *Titanic*. © Jonathan Reeve JR19999f27 1912.

46. 1.40am *Titanic* settles to forward stack, breaks between stacks. © Jonathan Reeve JR2197b98p201BL 1912.

47. To the amazement of the awed watchers in the lifeboats, the doomed vessel remained in an uprighr position for a time estimated at five minutes. © J & C McCutcheon Collection.

48. Lifeboats pull away from the sinking ship. *Titanic* starts to point skyward before her dive into the abyss. © Amberley Archive.

49. 1.50am *Titanic's* forward end floats then sinks. Jack Thayer (first class passenger, Boat B) was one of a number of survivors to describe the ship breaking in two as she sank. Sketch 4 of 6 of the series of illustrations drawn aboard *Carpathia* clearly show the two halves. It would be over seventy years before Thayer was proved right when the wreck was discovered resting on the seabed in two halves. © Jonathan Reeve JR2198b98p201TR 1912.

50. 2.00am Stern section of *Titanic* pivots and swings over spot where forward section sank. © Jonathan Reeve JR2199b98p201MR 1912.

51. *c*.2.15am Final position in which *Titanic* stayed for 5 minutes before the final plunge. © Jonathan Reeve JR2200b98p201BR 1912.

52. Colonel Gracie was in the water for a short while, being sucked down with the ship but luckily escaping the suction as she sank. He found himself some distance from an upturned collapsible boat, and, with a few, others, successfully managed to remain on the collapsible until taken into lifeboat 12 later that morning. © J & C McCutcheon Collection.

53. One of *Titanic's* lifeboats. © J & C McCutcheon Collection.

54. One of *Titanic's* lifeboats approaches the *Carpathia*. © Jonathan Reeve JR2014f42 1912.

55. Lifeboat 14 towing collapsable D. © Jonathan Reeve JR2015f43.

56. *Titanic* survivors in collapsable lifeboat D. © Jonathan Reeve JR2016f44 1912.

57. The Countess of Rothes (first class passenger, lifeboat 8) was from Prinknash Abbey, in Gloucestershire, where a memorial exists to the *Titanic*. © J & C McCutcheon.

58 & 59. *Titanic* passengers coming aboard the *Carpathia*. © Jonathan Reeve JR2108f98 1912 & JR2109f99 1912.

60. The survivors reached the *Carpathia* early next morning and were hauled aboard the gallant Cunarder. The youngest, Millvina Dean was pulled up in a sack. © J & C McCutcheon.

61. *Titanic* lifeboat alongside the *Carpathia*. The gangway doors are open to facilitate access. © J & C McCutcheon.

62, 63 & 64. Groups of *Titanic* survivors aboard rescue ship *Carpathia*. © Jonathan Reeve JR2090f80 1912, JR2023f53 1912 & JR2077f67 1912.

65. Groups of *Titanic* survivors aboard rescue ship *Carpathia*: George Harder and his wife Dorothy Harder (first class passengers, both rescued on lifeboat 5). The woman weeping, with hand to her face, is Clara Hays (first class passenger, lifeboat 3) her husband Charles M. Hays perished. When the cry came to get in the lifeboats the Harders, thinking there was no danger, jumped in the first boat lowered. © Jonathan Reeve JR2129f119 1912.

66. Captain Arthur Henry Rostron who rushed his ship *Carpathia* to the rescue of *Titanic's* survivors and brought them to New York. © Jonathan Reeve JR2120f110 1912.

67. The Cunard Line steamship *Carpathia* which heard the wireless call of distress from the *Titanic* and was the first to reach the scene of the disaster and take on board survivors. © Jonathan Reeve JR2135f125 1912.

68. Arrival of the *Carpathia* into New York on Thursday 18 April 1912. *Carpathia* dropped off the empty *Titanic* lifeboats at Pier 59, as property of the White Star Line, before unloading the survivors at Pier 54 where thousands of friends and relatives of the survivors were waiting. © Jonathan Reeve JR2008f36 1912.

69. P.A.S. Franklin, White Star Line Vice President. Yet, when the New York office of the White Star Line was informed that *Titanic* was in trouble, White Star Line Vice President P.A.S. Franklin announced 'We place absolute confidence in the *Titanic*. We believe the boat is unsinkable.' By the time Franklin spoke those words *Titanic* was at the bottom of the ocean. © Jonathan Reeve JR2098f88 1912.

70. Newspaper headline, Tuesday 16 April 1912. © Jonathan Reeve JR2005f33 1912.

71. A contemporary newspaper depiction of the location of the sinking of the *Titanic* and positions of other ships in the area. © Jonathan Reeve JR1993f21 1912.

72. Getting *Titanic* news. White Star Office, April 1912. © Jonathan Reeve JR2076f66 1912.

73. A photograph of Mrs Benjamin Guggenheim leaving the White Star offices in New York after trying to get news of her husband. He had dressed in his best before going down with the ship. © W.B Bartlett & the Amberley Archive.

74. Seeking information about lost relatives and friends at the office of the steamship company in New York. © Jonathan Reeve JR2124f114 1912.

75. Interior of the Cunard Line pier all cleared out ready to receive the survivors of the *Titanic* on arrival of the *Carpathia*, where they were met by relatives, doctors and nurses. © Jonathan Reeve JR2131f121 1912.

76. Crowd awaiting survivors from the *Titanic* 18 April 1912. © Jonathan Reeve JR2079f69 1912.

77. The *Titanic's* 13 surviving lifeboats in New York. Their nameplates and White Star flags were removed and the lifeboats disappeared. © Jonathan Reeve JR2117f107 1912.

78. Harold Bride (lifeboat B), surviving wireless operator of the *Titanic*, with feet bandaged, being carried up ramp of ship. He was washed off the deck of the *Titanic* just as it sank but managed to attach himself to the upturned hull of Collapsible B. © Jonathan Reeve JR2027f57 1912.

79. A happier picture of the second class child passengers French brothers Michel (age 4) and Edmond Navratil (age 2) in the care of fellow *Titanic* survivor, Margaret Hays. Miss Hays escaped on lifeboat 7 but volunteered once on board *Carpathia* to care for the 'orphans' as she could speak fluent French. They escaped the sinking ship in Collapsible D, their father perished. © Jonathan Reeve JR2125f115 1912.

80. Stuart Collett (second class passenger, lifeboat 9) one of the *Titanic* survivors arriving in New York on the *Carpathia*. © Jonathan Reeve JR2087f77 1912.

81. Frederick Fleet (lifeboat 6), Lookout on the *Titanic* who spotted the iceberg. © Jonathan Reeve JR2099f89 1912.

82. Newspaper headline, Friday 19 April 1912. © Jonathan Reeve JR2009f37 1912.

83. A contemporary picture lionising the bravery of the men on the *Titanic*. The myth of male sacrifice developed as the world tried to make sense of the disaster. In practice, some men were much more heroic than others. © W.B Bartlett & the Amberley Archive.

84. A drawing from Punch which was dedicated to the 'brave men' who perished in the disaster. Britannia looks on as a grieving woman tries to cope with the immensity of the tragedy. In practice, nearly 50 first class male passengers survived, most controversially Bruce Ismay. © W.B Bartlett & the Amberley Archive.

85. The Whited Sepulchre, a contemporary cartoon weighing up the *Titanic's* luxuries against the lives of some of her prominent passengers. © W.B Bartlett & the Amberley Archive.

86. *Which? fate or economy in life boats?* by W. A. Rogers (1854-1931) published in *New York Herald*, 17 April 1912. © Jonathan Reeve JR2101f91 1912.

87. Photo shows Captain Arthur Rostron and officers of *Carpathia* next to the silver loving cup presented to him in May 1912 by survivors of the *Titanic* in recognition of his heroism in their rescue. © Jonathan Reeve JR2105f95 1912.

88. Senate Investigating Committee questioning Harold Cottam at the Waldorf Astoria 29 May 1912. Harold Cottam, wireless operator on the *Carpathia* on the night of the *Titanic* struck an iceberg. It was he who alerted Captain Rostron who turned round the ship and put on all possible speed, and the *Carpathia* was the first ship on the scene of the tragedy. © Jonathan Reeve JR2071f61 1912.

89. First class passenger, Madeleine Astor (lifeboat 4). The eighteen year old bride of the millionaire John Astor who went down with the *Titanic* was pregnant at the time of the sinking and went on to give birth to a John Astor's son in August 1912. At one stage whilst waiting on the boat deck, the Astors retired to the gym and sat on the mechanical horses. © Jonathan Reeve JR2130f120 1912.

90. The Musicians Memorial in Southampton; this photograph is of a replica, the original was destroyed by a Luftwaffe bombing raid in the Second World War. © W.B Bartlett & the Amberley Archive.

91. The 'unsinkable' Margaret 'Molly' Brown (first class passenger, lifeboat 6). © Jonathan Reeve JR2088f78 1912.

92. The *Titanic* memorial a granite statue in Washington DC that honours the men who gave their lives so that women and children might be saved. © Jonathan Reeve JR2097f87 1912.

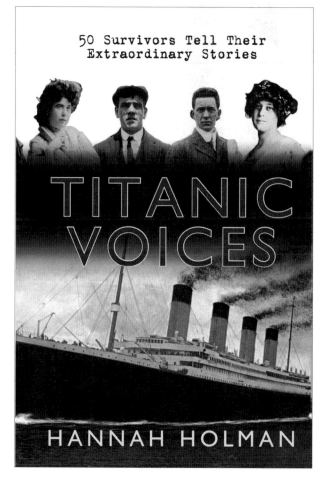